Emotional Intelligence for Leadership

4 Week Booster Plan to Increase Your Self-Awareness, Assertiveness and Your Ability to Manage People at Work

Jonatan Slane

© **Copyright 2019 - All rights reserved.**

The content contained within this book may not be reproduced, duplicated or transmitted without direct written permission from the author or the publisher.

Under no circumstances will any blame or legal responsibility be held against the publisher, or author, for any damages, reparation, or monetary loss due to the information contained within this book. Either directly or indirectly.

Legal Notice:

This book is copyright protected. This book is only for personal use. You cannot amend, distribute, sell, use, quote or paraphrase any part, or the content within this book, without the consent of the author or publisher.

Disclaimer Notice:

Please note the information contained within this document is for educational and entertainment purposes only. All effort has been executed to present accurate, up to date, and reliable, complete information. No warranties of any kind are declared or implied. Readers acknowledge that the author is not engaging in the rendering of legal, financial, medical or professional advice. The content within this book has been derived from various sources. Please consult a licensed professional before attempting any techniques outlined in this book.

By reading this document, the reader agrees that under no circumstances is the author responsible for any losses, direct or indirect, which are incurred as a result of the use of information contained within this document, including, but not limited to, — errors, omissions, or inaccuracies.

Hello Fellow Leader,

As a (soon-to-be) leader you are looking for ways to improve yourself in the most valuable areas.

The higher your Emotional Intelligence, the better..

- and higher your self-awareness
- your view and vision on your goals and goals of your organization
- your decision making, you make decisions based on sound logic instead on emotions
- your communication skills, smoother communication both 1-to-1 as in groups
- your negotiation skills

Which means better personal results and a both smoother and faster career- and salary development

So, don´t wait longer to receive ´The 4 Week Emotional Intelligence Booster Program´ in PDF format as well, by clicking the link below:

http://eiforleadership.businessleadershipplatform.com/

Print the document and put it in visible place, so you can improve your Emotional Intelligence daily.

Let´s get started ...

Enjoy,

Jonatan

Table of Contents

INTRODUCTION	11
PART I: UNDERSTANDING THE FOUNDATION: HUMAN EMOTIONS	17
ADVANCED COMBINATION EMOTIONS	21
WHY DO WE EXPERIENCE EMOTIONS?	22
EMOTIONAL RESPONSE VS. LOGIC AND DECISION-MAKING	23
CHAPTER 1: THE EQ MODELS	25
1. THE ABILITY MODEL	25
2. MIXED MODEL	27
3. TRAIT MODEL	28
CONCLUSION	29
CHAPTER 2: INTROSPECTION	31
EMOTIONAL SELF-REGULATION AND SELF-CONTROL	32
A REAL-LIFE EXAMPLE OF SELF-REGULATION	34
HOW TO MANAGE NEGATIVE BEHAVIORS AND EXERT POSITIVE RESPONSES	36
CONCLUSION	38
CHAPTER 3: EXTROSPECTION	39
RECOGNIZING EMOTIONS ON OTHERS	39
THE DIFFERENCE BETWEEN EMPATHY AND SYMPATHY	40
EXAMPLE OF EMPATHY	41
HAVING SOCIAL SKILLS	43
READING OTHERS' EMOTIONS	44
HOW TO LEVERAGE POSITIVE EMOTIONS IN PEOPLE	45
HOW TO DEAL WITH NEGATIVE EMOTIONS IN PEOPLE	46

CONCLUSION	49 |//

PART II: INTRODUCTION — 51

FOUR WEEK EMOTION INTELLIGENCE BOOSTER PROGRAM — 51

CHAPTER 4: WEEK 1: INTRO- BASICS- SELF-AWARENESS — 53

HOW DO YOU RECOGNIZE THE EMOTIONS AND FEELINGS WITHIN YOURSELF?	53
NEGATIVE EMOTIONAL REACTION EXAMPLE 1:	54
POSITIVE EMOTIONAL RESPONSE: EXAMPLE #1:	57
NEGATIVE EMOTIONAL RESPONSE EXAMPLE #2:	60
POSITIVE EMOTIONAL RESPONSE #2:	62
CONCLUSION	64

CHAPTER 5: WEEK 2: BASICS OF SELF-CONTROL — 69

ABOUT EMOTIONAL REGULATION	70
1. LABEL YOUR EMOTION	71
2. LETTING GO	72
3. SELF-CARE	74
4. BE POSITIVE	76
5. ALLOW YOURSELF TO ENJOY LIFE	78
6. WORRY LESS	80
7. NOTICE WHEN YOUR EMOTIONS START TO GET OUT OF HAND	82
8. HIT YOUR "PAUSE" BUTTON AND STOP YOURSELF	83
CONCLUSION	85

CHAPTER 6: WEEK 3: INTRO: BASICS TO RECOGNIZING EMOTIONS IN OTHERS

91

RECOGNIZING EMOTIONS IN A PERSON: THE BASIC EMOTIONS	94
SADNESS	95
FEAR	97

ANGER	98
DISGUST	100
SURPRISE	101
MORE COMPLEX EMOTIONS AT WORK	103
HAPPY FOR SOMEONE VS. JEALOUSY	103
AWE	105
SHAME OR EMBARRASSMENT	107
CONTEMPT	109
ANTICIPATION	111
RELIEF	112
SATISFACTION	114
THE POWER OF VERBAL COMMUNICATION: IT'S ALL IN THE VOICE	115
CONCLUSION	118
CHAPTER 7- WEEK 4: INTRO: BASICS: SOCIAL SKILL	**125**
LEARNING TO REACT THE PROPER WAY	125
DEVELOPING GOOD LISTENING SKILLS	128
GENUINE EMPATHY	137
UNDERSTANDING STRESS	141
HOW TO DEAL WITH COMPLAINTS: IS IT VALID OR INVALID COMPLAINING?	144
HOW TO CREATE A POSITIVE ATMOSPHERE	146
HOW TO GIVE THE CORRECT GUIDANCE	148
WHEN TO GET MAD? WHEN NOT TO GET MAD? HOW TO GET MAD IN A CIVILIZED AND PRODUCTIVE WAY?	150
CONCLUSION	**161**
BIBLIOGRAPHY	**167**

Introduction

Everyone wants to improve their job, to get better at what they do. It's a part of what makes us human. We desire innovation and the ability to overcome unique challenges. And that involves investing our entire selves into what we do. Perhaps, you are looking for ways to improve and develop further at work. There are many ways that we can improve our various situations by having the right attitude and work habits to promote productivity.

One of the ways of developing productivity is by becoming emotionally mature in handling different situations. We have to develop emotional intelligence, to know how people are feeling at work, and think of different ways that we can improve the workspace at the office and promote worker happiness and satisfaction. That is one of our responsibilities as managers. It is to find ways that we can engage our employees and bring them to higher productivity and achievement so that we can promote our products and services and allow our customers to be happy. Therefore, it is crucial that we find ways to connect with our workers emotional needs and it is helpful to have emotional intelligence.

There are different benefits to developing one's emotional

intelligence. For one, managers can learn to handle their teams better. Managers can learn what motivates their team and how they become emotionally sensitive to different issues. They can also learn how to handle demanding colleagues, who can be hard to deal with their emotional reactions and constant negativity at work. Additionally, emotional intelligence allows managers to create a working environment, where employees are developing positive and meaningful relationships with their peers. For employees, the benefits of gauging emotional intelligence can be helpful, because they can use social skills, the right emotions at the right time. They can then get things like pay raise or a promotion so that they can live happier lives. Finding the right motivations is a critical factor in increasing satisfaction in different people. Therefore, it is one of the best ways of getting people to perform well at work.

The history of emotional intelligence research began with Peter Salovey and John D. Mayer. These two researchers created the term emotional intelligence. They started a research program to highlight different measures of emotional intelligence in people. In one study, they discovered that when a group of people saw an emotionally-stirring film, those that had a higher emotional sensitivity were able to recover much more quickly than the ones that didn't. Within another study, people who were able to assess emotions accurately were able to adjust to changes within their social life and build positive social networks.

In the 1990s, Daniel Goleman wrote a book, *Emotional Intelligence* (1995), which argued that emotional intelligence is more important than IQ in determining the success of an individual. He regularly coaches others about the different competencies involved in relationship management. And he says that when someone focuses on improving their awareness of emotions, they will be able to see better health benefits and improvement in their relationships. The research of Daniel Coleman has helped people as they have discovered the importance of emotional intelligence and how it can help develop a sense of community within different social circles.

This book is called Emotional Intelligence for Leadership, and it is going to show you all the different ways of developing emotional intelligence that will help your team to thrive with happy employees who will produce excellent work in your company. We will talk about various aspects of emotional intelligence, including self-awareness, self-regulation, social awareness, social skills, and assertiveness to become more productive. Having all of this knowledge will help you to become a better manager and to get more done with less time and energy. Within this book, we will give examples of the work environment with different stories to illustrate our points and provide a real-life scenario that you can understand completely. We want to allow this material to come alive as you are reading it, so you will have fun and learn a lot in the process.

In our opinion, success is less determined by IQ (intelligence quotient) than it is by EQ (emotional quotient). You can have a high IQ and have a low EQ. The thing is, emotionally sensitive people can make a big difference in the workplace. They can foster a sense of community in others and witness the success of different colleagues in a company. A survey by Career Builder in 2011 found that 71% of hiring managers said that they thought an employee's EQ was more important than their IQ. Also, 75% said that they would promote a person with a high EQ.

Moreover, more than half (59%) reported that they would not hire a person who had a high IQ and a low EQ. Employers use EQ as a way of assessing if an individual has leadership potential and can make an impact in the workplace. It is something that employers want in their candidates, to meet the needs of the other workers. It is also something that employers can use to build effective relationships with their employees. This aspect also helps them to develop their mindset in how they can be active managers and have a good relationship with their employees.

There are two parts to this book. In the first part, we'll talk about emotions and self-awareness. We will discuss the basic human feelings, as well as the more advanced ones. We will also go into depth about EQ and what it means. We will even talk about the implications of EQ for your private life and social life. In the second part of the book, we will give you a four-week emotional intelligence booster plan, which will provide you with a project to work on. We will provide you with different strategies to work on for different emotions so that you can train yourself in emotional intelligence. We will advise you to work on it one emotion at a time so that you can hone the craft of emotional regulation and awareness of others, which will make you more productive at work and also help you in your relationships with others in your company.

We believe that this book will give you all the tools you need to succeed in emotional intelligence and provide productivity and joy in your company while satisfying you, your colleagues, employees, and clients.

Part I: Understanding the Foundation: Human Emotions

Emotions are an essential part of who we are as humans. They are a fundamental part of our framework and make-up and demonstrate the depths of our feelings and thoughts. They influence how we live our lives and have meaningful interactions with others. Our emotions powerfully impact how we act in our lives, and they can quickly overtake us and push us to do actions that are entirely off the edge. The people who surround we can influence our emotions. When a person has pain or anxiety within a problematic relationship, a friend can help encourage them in their lives to go forward. Another example of emotional responses to situations includes gossip. Whenever people gossip about another, other people may have a negative attitude or feeling toward that person. Also, a person who is always negative and exhibits feelings of anger or frustration can affect others around him or her.

Throughout history, psychologists have tried to classify the emotions that people experience. One psychologist, Paul Eckman, named six basic emotions that are experienced by people in all cultures. Let's look at these emotions here in more detail.

1. Happiness

Happiness is the experience of feelings of joy, gratification, satisfaction, and contentment. There has been extensive research carried out about happiness with the advent of positive psychology. Most people want to live happy lives. Happiness is characterized by different expressions such as smiling, body language in a relaxed way, or a positive and pleasant tone in speaking (Cherry, 2018). Happiness is one of the basic human emotions, but people in this world tend to make it a lot more complicated than it should be. They think that gaining material possessions, acquiring wealth, or having a beautiful home or car, or having a high-paying job will bring happiness to people.

Research has demonstrated that the experience of happiness influences your physical and mental health. Happiness has been linked with longer life expectancy and increased overall satisfaction with life. On the other hand, unhappiness has led people to experience more loneliness, anxiety, and depression.

2. **Sadness**

Sadness is an emotion that involves a person feeling in a low mood state with feelings of grief, disappointment, and other feelings. It is something that a person experiences from time to time. However, during periods where it's at its worst, it becomes a depressive episode. Sadness is an emotion that can be either a passing emotion that includes crying or getting upset, but it can become more serious whenever people experience intense sadness due to a variety of factors. That said, sadness can lead people to avoid people, self-medicate with alcohol or illegal drugs, or dwell on negative thoughts. These types of compulsive behaviors can easily become addictions that will make a person stay in a low or depressive state.

3. **Disgust**

Disgust is another one of the six basic emotions. It involves turning away from something that a person finds revolting or unbearable. Disgust usually includes a physical component, including vomiting, wrinkling your nose, or moving your upper lip. Feelings of disgust arise from different things, including an unbearable smell, taste, or sight. Some people believe that this emotion originated from the reactions to foods that have gone bad which might harm a person. When a person eats a food that has gone bad, he usually responds with disgust.

4. **Surprise**

Surprise is often a fleeting sensation that a person feels whenever he is startled by something surprising. It can be a surprise birthday party or someone that scares you unexpectedly. You may feel positive or negative feelings about surprise. Surprised expressions include widened eyes, opening one's mouth, raising the eyebrows, jumping back from a situation, gasping, or screaming. Furthermore, surprise is an emotion, which can trigger a fight-or-flight response (Cherry, 2018). In this case, the person either wants to stay and fight the emotional response or leave the situation. Surprise can have a powerful effect on how a person reacts to different situations and lives his life.

5. **Fear**

Fear is an emotion that a person experiences when faced with some danger or experience of a fight or flight response. In this type of emotion, the person becomes tense, his heart rate increases and a person has a primal instinct response to a situation of either staying and fighting within the situation or leaving the scene. The fight or flight response is useful in helping protect people from danger or threats to a person's safety and physical wellbeing.

6. Anger

Anger is an emotion that involves feelings of frustration, hostility, and aggression toward another person. It can also be part of a person's fight and flight response to a situation. When a person is moved by anger, he will have expressions of frowning or glaring at a person. He will want to move away from another person. Also, he may yell at another person. A physical response includes turning red in the face or sweating. Anger can lead a person to act out in violent ways, such as striking another, kicking, or throwing and destroying things. Many people think of anger as a negative emotion; however, it can have some benefits, because it can make people seek justice in situations where there is the unjust treatment of others. People who are motivated by a cause can take action united in their anger at a given situation. On the other hand, anger can be harmful and cause significant damage to a person's health. It has been linked to different diseases, including heart disease and diabetes. Finally, some angry people engage in risky and harmful activities such as aggressive driving, alcohol, or smoking cigarettes.

Advanced Combination Emotions

In addition to the underlying emotions, there are other advanced emotions, which are combinations of a few feelings. For example, the emotion optimism is a combination of anticipation and joy. Its advanced opposite is disappointment. Optimism is a positive emotion that involves happiness, but it also consists of anticipating the future and looking to the possibilities. It is much more than mere happiness; it has a forward component that involves the future. Another emotion that is a combination of different emotions is awe, which is a combo of fear and surprise. When you are in awe of the situation, you stand both amazed and in fear of something. Perhaps, this is a natural wonder outside, or it is a fear of God that a person may have. To be in awe is a complex emotion. Another combination of emotion is contempt, which is a combination of disgust and anger. It involves a certain level of anger against something but also a disgusted reaction to a person for doing something wrong or upsetting. Another combination of emotion is remorse, which involves a mixture of sadness and disgust. When a person is remorseful, he is regretful of his actions and feels both sad and disgusted at the same time. So, it also has a layer of complexity to it. Finally, love is a complex emotion involving both happiness and trust. A person feels happy with another person, but also trusting and accepting of another, so it is something that has a combination of feelings.

As you can see, the advanced combination emotions have a lot more to them than what meets the eye. They combine the effects of at least two emotions. For example, a high school student may feel disappointed when he gets a bad grade on a chemistry test after having had studied for 10 hours for it. He feels both sad from it but also a bit surprised at the score from it.

Why Do We Experience Emotions?

We experience emotional changes based on our environment, a change inside of us, or both. Emotions change rather quickly and can last from a few minutes to a few hours to a few days. They depend on the situation a person is in. The function of an emotion is to bring something to our attention and get us to produce a response (Josh Clark). Psychologists don't agree as to whether it is an involuntary response or if it is based on a judgment that a person makes based on evaluating their situation.

Emotions motivate us in our lives. They incite us to change and action. For example, when we feel disgusted over what our government is doing about immigration regulation, we feel incited to petition for change. Another example is with anger. When we are angry, we feel compelled to fight and stand up for what is right. Alternatively, when we're fearful, we want to run away from a dangerous situation. Emotions motivate us to stay right where we are and enjoy our lives, in particular, if we are enjoying our lives. However, they can also produce in us a response that can be either positive or negative to a given situation.

Additionally, emotions enable us to empathize with others. When we see someone grieving, we feel for them and want to comfort them with our presence and safety. Thus, emotions enable us to form strong connections with others within a social context. All the basic emotions can be worn on a person's face. As a result, they are overtly present to others when we are talking to them. Emotions then become social cues that we use to get our points across and communicate about different matters.

Emotional Response vs. Logic and Decision-Making

You may not realize it but many of our decisions are motivated by emotional responses, rather than by logic, and this can lead to different kinds of situations. A person may have just received his paycheck and get excited by the money in his bank account and then go on a spending spree and use up a lot of his money and then get into trouble with his finances toward the end of the month. Because he was motivated to spend his hard-earned money on frivolous things. It was driven from an emotion of excitement of receiving the money in his bank account. Consequently, he loses his money and may become sad or disheartened.

Another example of an emotional reaction is that a government elects a strong right-winged politician at the time when there is intense terrorism, and people want to elect someone who can crack down on immigration and protect the citizens. People are motivated by fear to elect the politician, who will protect them from terrorism by trying to enact laws that will protect border control. People are fearful and thus want to choose a politician, who would have a strong stance on immigration. In the 2016 election, there was a lot of emotional motivation to the decisions made by people, based on their fears and anxieties. This incited them to elect people such as Donald Trump. Not to get political. However, it is true that people become very emotional when they talk about political things.

On the other hand, a person may be motivated by a rational decision to save money when receiving a bonus. Instead of responding with an emotional reaction of going out and spending all the money on things, the person may put the money into a savings account, knowing he will use it to spend on a vacation or new car. That would be the logical and rational decision to make in that situation. For the second situation with the election, the people would make their decision to vote, not based on fear, but instead, they would decide by looking at the platforms of the candidates, analyzing the perspectives and policies, and in other ways. Consequently, they would make their decisions based on the empirical evidence available and not based on their emotions.

It is easy to make decisions based on our emotions because they can be strong and powerful and influence our behaviors. However, it is crucial that we pay attention to how we can respond to situations less emotionally and more with logic and rational thinking, because if we are not careful, we may do things that we regret and get ourselves into trouble. Therefore, it is vital that we have both emotional sensitivity and rational thinking to make the best decisions in our lives. It is also true that emotions can lead us to make the right decisions, if we are in a distressful situation, for example with a fight or flight response.

To conclude, emotions are an essential part of what makes us human. They drive us to action and response. Although they are powerful and influential, they can lead to adverse reactions and consequences. It is vital that we find ways of dealing with our emotions that are constructive and useful to our wellbeing and that of others.

Chapter 1: The EQ Models

Emotional intelligence is the ability to "perceive, control, and evaluate emotions." The term was made famous by a man named Daniel Goleman, but Michael Beldoch coined it in 1964. Emotional intelligence is a person's ability to monitor one's own and other people's emotions, to distinguish between different emotions, and to use information about the emotions to guide a person's thinking and behavior. To make the concept of emotional intelligence clearer and more logical, three models were developed, the ability model, mixed model, and the trait model.

1. The Ability Model

Salovey and Mayer developed this model. They said that emotional intelligence enables a person to think about emotions to enhance their reasoning skills. It discusses a person's abilities to gauge and understand people's emotions and to regulate them. This model says that there are several different abilities.

   a. Perceiving emotions. With this ability, the person can read another's emotions throughout both verbal and nonverbal communication.

   b. Reasoning with emotions. With this skill, a person can reason through different situations and figure out how to solve a problem using the emotions. It enables a person to be attentive to what is going on around them and react appropriately based on their surroundings.

c. Understanding emotions. Emotions are complex and they have many different meanings that help us to understand how a person is going and how they are reacting to a given situation. Emotions themselves have different colors, and they have interactions with each other frequently. Because each emotion is connected to a specific behavior or response, you can deduce why a person acts the way they do in a given situation. For example, if a person's angry, their reasoning might be that they were not treated fairly. The possible action associated with this emotion would be to get revenge, withdraw, or attack another in this situation. As you can see, emotions are linked together.

d. Managing emotions. In the ability model, the person must learn how to control his or her responses to the various emotions that he or she perceives or experiences in his or her life.

2. Mixed Model

Daniel Goleman created 25 emotional characteristics, which include many different aspects of the emotions, including teamwork and collaboration, service orientation, and motivation for success (Slaazar, 2017). It's called a mixed model because it includes not only information about emotional intelligence but also aspects related to personality traits. Here are some examples of how this is used.

1. **Self-awareness**: This is the ability to recognize that you are experiencing emotion at the time of speaking. We have to acknowledge how we are feeling at a given time and know how to manage our complex emotional patterns. Self-awareness involves two key aspects:

    A. Self-confidence in a person's unique abilities

    B. Emotional awareness in understanding a person's emotions and their effects

2. **Self-regulation**: To deal with our issues of regulation, we have to self-regulate through doing activities that will help us to face stress and conflicting emotions. Examples include walking, prayer, and meditation. Self-regulation involves a certain level of personal integrity, creativity, adaptability, and conscientiousness.

3. **Motivation**: To do something well, you have to have a goal in mind. Motivation enables a person to pursue his or her dream. Positive thinking is an integral part of this kind of ability. Within this ability, a person can be optimistic and confident, ready to tackle any challenges, in pursuit of his or her goal.

4. **Empathy**: This is a person's ability to relate to the emotions of others and understanding how they feel. When a person feels compassion for another, they can understand and help others who are in need. They can also fulfill their requirements by helping to encourage them in whatever they are dealing with.

5. **Social skills**: For this skill, you need to be able to work and collaborate with others and communicate effectively. In addition, you will need to know how to resolve conflict and build relationships and rapport with others around you.

3. Trait Model

Petrides and his colleagues developed the trait model in 2009. It differs from the previous two models in that it shows that people have emotional traits or self-perceptions that are part of a person's unique personality (Salazar 2017). Emotional intelligence is an individual's ability to examine himself or herself in light of his or her emotional skills, as mentioned in the ability model. The traits that a person has are based on a person's self-perception but are not measured by any scientific way. This model has to explore all the facets of a person's personality before it can be useful in evaluating a person's emotional intelligence.

Conclusion

To sum up, each of these models is important to getting a person to realize the ability to monitor and recognize the emotions that they are experiencing. It also helps the person to have a higher degree of self-acceptance and self-awareness of factors, such as personality and ability to understand the experience of emotions. The models help a person to deal with the complex feelings that they have from day-to-day and understand how their personality affects their emotional responses to the given stimuli.

Chapter 2: Introspection

In this chapter, we are going to look at introspection as we look at ourselves and how we experience various emotions in our lives.

Within our emotion cycles, we have to look deep within ourselves to see how our personality affects our emotions. According to the preceding models we have looked at, personality shapes a big way that we can deal with our emotions. Moreover, one way our personality manifests itself is through our self-confidence and self-esteem.

When we have negative self-esteem, this impacts how we experience our emotions. Also, when a person is negative all the time, his or her emotions will manifest themselves in negative ways. Therefore, it is crucial to recognize that a person with higher emotional intelligence will recognize that their self-esteem impacts the way they view themselves and how they experience emotional cycles from day to day.

When a person has positive self-esteem, he or she will experience emotional cycles more positively, because they will be comfortable with themselves and not feel the need to worry about aspects that they have not accepted about their personality and attributes, and such. People with positive self-esteem have a higher degree of self-acceptance and will be more apt to forgive themselves for mistakes they have made or offenses that they have made against others. This also impacts how a person will experience their emotions throughout the day.

As we go through introspection of ourselves, we have to ask ourselves, how do we know that we are experiencing emotions. It takes a degree of self-awareness that is important to figure out what kind of emotions we are having at a given time. To access this self-awareness, we need to think about how we respond to a given situation and assess whether or not that was motivated by some emotional reaction or if it was based on logic. For that, you have to examine the facts of a given situation and assess what they are. One way to track how you are doing with your emotional awareness is by keeping an emotions journal. Every day, you can write in it how you are feeling at different moments in the day and highlight what happened. Think about what events happened that day, which may have triggered your emotions and provided you with some powerful response to the given stimuli.

Emotional Self-Regulation and Self-Control

Children must learn how to manage their emotions and usually do this in a safe and supportive environment. However, adults must control their emotions alone and have to have a high degree of self-control to function as productive individuals in society. In particular, an adult must deal with the negative emotions that can easily overwhelm and discourage, including anger, anxiety, and frustration, to prevent any negative responses that can result in regrettable behavior. Self-regulation enables a person to recognize the stimuli that are causing a person to act out on their emotions and helps them to keep them in check and respond in appropriate ways that will help them in a given situation. There are different techniques that a person can practice to improve in this area of emotional wellness. That includes meditation, mindfulness, and other ways of managing stress. With emotional regulation, a person learns how to reduce the intensity of the experience of emotions. For example, a person who is mourning the loss of a loved one might recall a happy memory that helps them cope with the sadness that they are experiencing. Alternatively, an angry person can think of happy thoughts or amusing things that will help them to laugh off the situation. Emotional regulation involves an element of distracting the person from the situation to cope and to aid in response to a given situation. It is also known as "down-regulation," which is useful for playing down the emotions to calm and soothe a person into responding in appropriate and constructive ways.

Additionally, emotional regulation is used to control impulsive behaviors, such as spending too much money. We all know people who buy impulsively on the Internet and then lose money because they have spent too much. Everyone has the same emotional experience of receiving a paycheck and then wanting to buy merchandise afterward. Emotional regulation helps a person to recognize the excitement and respond to it in an appropriate way that does not result in a harmful overspending habit that can lead from the given situation. If a person recognizes that they need to pay bills and cannot resort to overspending, they will stop and not spend on that next handbag or pair of shoes, but rather keep the money safely.

On the other side is up-regulation of emotions, which plays up the emotions, based on a given situation, including times of distress, for example, when there is a fire or a danger that surrounds a person. This type of regulation is essential whenever there is a presence of danger and initiates a "fight or flight" response. It is used to give a person a degree of anxiety or excitement that is appropriate in responding to a situation and helps a person to escape or help others get out of a situation.

A Real-Life Example of Self-Regulation

Emily was a high-strung individual. She was a hardworking administrative assistant. She always did her job and to a high standard and yet she always felt inadequate and that she could do better. Emily had become quite the workaholic type, who would constantly work on projects and never stop in the evening. Every day she would think about work, and she had no work-life balance in her life. Therefore, she was tired every day and then the one thing that was getting her through the day was caffeine, and that was causing her to lose sleep because she was taking too much of it in her system.

Although she was quite organized, Emily tended to procrastinate on one or two items on her agenda, especially the things that she didn't want to do. One day, it was the management of her task app on the computer and things piled up on the task app. Then, it was her desk, which also started to accumulate things on it. After having procrastinated on these little items, Emily had a panic attack when she realized that she had forgotten a few of the tasks from her task app that should have been done yesterday. When she realized it, she was shocked and went into panic mode. It was so difficult for her at the time, she screamed and went crying to the ladies' room; it was a case of a nervous breakdown that she was having.

The thing is, however, Emily would have these cases of

nervous breakdowns once every few months and they would become pretty ugly. Emily realized that she was having a hard time, so she talked with one of her colleagues about what to do, and she learned some coping strategies for knowing how to handle her emotions and also how to avoid going into full-on panic mode.

Emily's colleague advised her to write down what it was that was making her stressed and feel that she was going over the edge. She needed to make notes about how she was feeling at the time so that she could refer back to them later. Then, she told her how to stop herself from going off into panic mode by diverting to something different and distracting from the situation. She also advised her to do meditation and practice mindfulness afterward. Emily later became more acutely aware of how she could handle her emotions and control herself before going off the edge with panic attacks.

After four months of therapy, Emily was able to come up with ways that she could manage her emotions better and then she was able to handle the various stressors that she had by writing things down, prioritizing what absolutely needed to be done on a given day, and doing things in an organized way.

How to Manage Negative Behaviors and Exert Positive Responses

The way to respond to negative emotions is simple; it's learning how to exercise a degree of self-control and try to ramp up the positive responses to the emotions. Rather than reacting to a situation, the person learns how to externalize their frustration or anxieties by focusing on what is positive in a given situation. For example, rather than getting into a shouting match with coworkers or swearing profusely, a person can use positive words to encourage someone else or externalize through writing their frustrations. Finding ways to be creative in getting out your emotional energy is essential because if you don't get it out some way, it is going to blow up and it won't be pretty. Therefore, it is vital that you find some good ways to do this and to be innovative in how you respond to different situations. Whenever you experience a negative emotion, you should recognize it as being the emotion you are having at a time, analyze it and see if it reflects the reality that you're in, and then choose an appropriate action that will be constructive and helpful. This won't always happen in a few minutes. It might happen instantaneously. The important thing is to train yourself how you are going to react rather than finding yourself still blowing up in a given situation and causing both strains to you and your relationships with others.

Positive responses are the best way to deal with the negative emotions we experience. You may have heard that you can cancel a negative with a positive. One positive word can infuse your life with a lot of positive energy and response to a given situation, while a negative word can give you a lot of stress and anxiety. Therefore, it is vital that you keep everything positive and uplifting for your health and wellbeing. One way to be more positive is to use motivation. This aspect allows you to focus on motivating yourself to be a better person by setting goals and by seeing the bright side of things. When you set a goal or target for yourself, you will always be looking to achieve something and will go after it with your energy. This will infuse your mind with positive energy that will make you feel good and will counter any of the negative thoughts that may enter your mind.

Practical Example

Let's give an example of how a person uses creativity to manage negative emotions and integrate positivity. Henry is a lazy worker, who always gets by with doing nothing. On most days, he arrives late to work, a bit hung over, tired, and smelling as if he had not taken a shower the night before. When he's working at the cafe, he always finds ways of sneaking out back to have a cigarette, because he's bored out of his mind. One day, he was out having a cigarette with a few colleagues, and he started out of the blue cursing his luck and saying "I suck. I can't believe that I live here in this place. I will never amount to anything. My life has no meaning! Sometimes, I don't give a _____ but today I really don't." Then, a coworker named Isaac from the cafe told him something very important.

Isaac told Henry, "Look, Henry, you've got to pull yourself together. You need to get a goal or vision for your life. I know you feel hopeless right now. However, I believe there is something that you can go for in your life, some kind of goal or dream that I want you to pursue. Do you think you can?" Henry said, "Nope. I have no dream or vision." Isaac replied:

"How about you do this? Write down things that you want in your life and think about how you can get those things and write down a goal that you want to achieve." Henry then wrote down some things that he wanted to do to get better in his life. That included stopping smoking and drinking and having a girlfriend. Isaac said: "see there, you do have something you want in your life. I know that you can accomplish these things if you really set out to do them." After this talk, Henry felt very happy, and he thought that he could take the necessary steps to stop smoking, take up a sport, and do some positive things.

So, what happened in this situation? Isaac, who is the inspirational motivator in this scenario, believed he could do something for Henry. He could instill in him an inspiration to have a dream. Henry was feeling hopeless, sad, and angry, all at the same time and then he felt happy after he had a dream and goal for the future, so it was a successful time.

Conclusion

To sum up, it is vital that you find creative ways of responding to negativity in your life, which includes positive emotional responses to the negative thoughts that may come across your mind. Looking further at yourself and having a high degree of self-awareness and acceptance will help you realize your natural tendencies, evaluate whether or not your emotional responses to situations are helpful or healthy, and come up with action plans or goals that will enable you to be more positive in responding to given situations that involve your emotions.

Chapter 3: Extrospection

Getting to know yourself and how you emotionally react to situations is an integral part of the process of self-awareness and knowledge. Equally important equally essential and valuable is getting to know about the emotions of other people and how they are feeling and reacting to different kinds of stimuli and situations. The opposite of introspection is extrospection, and within this type of awareness, a person can understand how people around them behave and interact with one another. There are different aspects of extrospection.

Recognizing Emotions on Others

The most basic fundamental way to understand people is by reading their emotions, which includes body language and facial expressions. People communicate a lot more than just with the words that they say, but also with how they speak, how they behave and demonstrate interest or disinterest in conversations. People will make eye contact, nod their head, give verbal cues and grunt and other signs of understanding, agreeing, and disagreeing. Within conversations, many different signs communicate the level of energy and interest. Learning to read how people accept or reject your words is an essential sign of emotional maturity. It is crucial to understand how a person is feeling when talking to them.

The Difference Between Empathy and Sympathy

Empathy is a way of feeling the different emotions of the people around you. It is a way in which a person can fully understand, accept, and identify with the person who is experiencing an emotion. Think about the person who is grieving the loss of their grandmother. You are in the position of having lost your grandmother or grandfather, and you know exactly how it feels to lose someone special to you. Therefore, it puts you in the position to counsel, listen to, and comfort the person who is going through this challenging stage of mourning the loss of a loved one. Empathy involves shared experiences that a person must feel the pain of another person, to completely identify with the other person. When a person says, "I feel you" or "I feel your pain," it is a sign of empathy and identification with another person, who is hurting somehow.

Another example is if a friend loses a job and has no money and is unable to pay his bills. You, who have already lost a job once and had no money at the time, can immediately identify with this person and offer to help him out. You feel empathy for your friend because you have been through the same or similar situation. Consequently, you can identify with the feelings and emotional responses of your friend. This puts you in the best position to comfort and restore your friend. Thus, you help him out by buying him a meal the day he lost his job, and you also might lend him some money, as well.

On the other hand, sympathy is when a person identifies a person's feelings of distress or suffering but is unable to know what a person is going through. It is somewhat like compassionate pity for someone in which a person may feel sorry for another but also comforts them. At the same time, they don't have the actual life experience that enables them to understand fully what another person is going through emotionally. An example is a doctor who is giving care to a patient who is suffering from cancer. Doctors have to be emotionally sensitive and aware to be competent and supportive caregivers.

Example of Empathy

Vicky always knew what it was like to be a proofreader and that it always involved looking at extensive data collections for long periods every day and staring in front of a computer. She was the supervisor of all the proofreaders within the editing company. There were several interns in that group, and she remembered what it was like to be on the job for the first time. She had squinted at the screen for long periods and sometimes had eye strain that she had to deal with, which was painful. Vicki also remembered the time when she completely misread a whole text and missed a lot of the errors in grammar on one page. This happened once when she was a young proofreader and had no experience in the job. She was mortified at the time and felt complete shame and remorse as a result of the experience. She feared for her career. She thought she might be fired over it. However, her supervisor told her it would be all right and that they could correct the mistake.

When Jason was first hired as a proofreader, he had no experience in the field and was feeling woefully inadequate and thought he would not be able to complete the assignments that he had. He had to proofread thousands of words per day, and it was so mentally and physically exhausting to look at two screens every day. He knew that it was a challenge to do that. And one day, it happened. He skipped a whole section of proofreading that had important data that had been either omitted or erroneous. The client who was in charge spotted the error and returned the document to the editing company, livid as a result of the problem. Jason's supervisor recognized it and played the middle man between the two, but she also came to Jason and said, you know Jason you made these mistakes and I need to follow-up with you about it. When Jason heard that he had made so many mistakes, he was also mortified and felt so bad. A lump descended into his throat, and he could hardly breathe. When he talked to Vicky, he was losing his energy and felt so bad about it. He was feeling shame and remorse, as a result of what he had done. However, then Vicky gave him the negative feedback that he had been waiting for her to unleash at him. As Vicky was giving the input, there was gentleness and tenderness in her voice that made it possible for her to share with him in a way that would be positive and uplifting. She made him feel a lot better because she had empathy for him. Vicki knew precisely how it was to be new to proofreading and to make mistakes in the work. Therefore, she was able to side with Jason and realized that he could do better next time. Vicki was an advocate for Jason and told the client that the proofreader was new and that it was his first time doing this type of assignment.

After that communication, the client came back with a note of understanding that showed empathy also with Jason and his first experience. It was a positive resolution to a difficult situation. This type of scenario is an example of emotional empathy. Vicky had compassion for Jason because she knew exactly how he felt and how he had a bad day. She also had compassion for Jason and knew that he could improve in the future if he applied himself. Jason also felt sorry for what he had done but was able to get better after that episode. All ended well.

Having Social Skills

A key aspect of developing sympathy or empathy with others is by improving your social skills. This means being in tune with how others are in your life. You're able to have better relationships with people through developing your interpersonal skills. If you want to make other people like you, you're going to have to know how people think, act, and behave. That also means understanding others' sense of humor and style of communication. Not everyone communicates the same way, so it is best to learn how to communicate effectively across different lines. When you have the social skills to help with communication, then you will be able to seamlessly do many things with others, which will strengthen relational ties and enable you to have fun in the process.

Social skills include the ability to relate to others and their interests. It means taking a vested interest in what others think and feel in their lives. Social people are always interested in what others have to say and have higher self-esteem. Because they exude self-confidence and are seeking to meet others with similar and unique interests, they know how to communicate their thoughts and feelings to others. Whereas, people without good social skills will struggle to find ways to relate to others and quickly get offended or hurt by others, especially when it comes to jokes and humorous things that they may not readily get.

A crucial part of interpersonal communication is knowing

how to relate to others' feelings and how they think and behave. The way to do this involves some getting to know others and their tastes. That said, it also takes some creative thinking. It is important to note how well you respond to people's emotions in times of conflict or other things.

Reading Others' Emotions

Reacting to others' emotions is a vital part of how you can make meaningful relationships. However, it is not always helpful. A lot of times, it is quite harmful. For example, a group of men arguing in a bar after having drunk a lot can result in some severe communication that may result in injury on both parties. One man might call another a dirty name, and the other man would get very angry and react in anger to the name-calling and make a violent turn to the evening. It could result in destructive behavior and physical injury. Emotional reactions in their worst form can occur in acts that are shameful and harmful. That was an example of the worst kind of emotional response.

However, what about reacting to other's sense of humor or jokes? Sometimes, people will make jokes or inter-racial slurs or different offensive remarks that can invoke anger in a person and cause a great deal of discord among people. Laughing has a way of bringing people together to enjoy an amusing joke; however, it can also be very offensive to some people and cause them to react in anger or frustration at the laughing person. This is where learning others' communication styles is very important. It is crucial that you find ways of relating to other people's emotions and sense of humor because that will be the way that you can make friends with others.

Also, you have to understand whenever others are feeling sad and how you can react to their sadness and provide comfort and support to them. In particular, when someone else is having a tough time at work or school and needs someone to comfort them, you can provide the necessary support that your friend needs because you are there for him or her and can do all things for them. Being a good friend involves sharing in the joys with your loved ones, as well as the challenging times. It requires a person to have maximum emotional sensitivity.

How to Leverage Positive Emotions in People

When you observe how people behave, you will notice how they act when they are experiencing positive or negative emotions. Usually, when a person is displaying a positive feeling, their faces will light up, they will smile or laugh, and there will generally be a positive, exuberant, and upbeat tone in their voice. Usually, positive people are entertaining to be around and can make you feel their positivity everywhere you go. They tend to give people lots of energy.

Moreover, when you're around a positive person, you will feel how they give their energy and help you experience warmth and joy in your life. The way to leverage positive emotion is how it has an impact on you personally. Does it give you energy and move you forward? Does it bring you excitement, anticipation, or joy? Then, it would be a more positive emotion that you would be experiencing from that person. Often, with positive people, you will want to get closer to them and spend more time with them. Positive people are great to be around, and they can help you improve your self-esteem and confidence.

How to Deal with Negative Emotions in People

On the other side of things are negative people. They bring us down. They always suck our energy and time and tear down all the positive energy that we may exude. Negative people radiate negative energy and emotions. Most of the time their energy is negative. Think of the Negative Nancy at the office who curses as soon as she arrives and complains about every little thing. She then causes other people to complain and gripe. Moreover, pretty soon, the whole office is filled with Negative Nancies and Neds. It is evident that negative emotions tend to zap people of energy. They also demoralize situations where people are perfectly content and happy because they cause people to doubt their ability to have a good time and enjoy their lives because they emphasize the negative. Emotional reactions such as anger also cause the person to become stressed and anxious, which ups the blood sugar and other things. It creates a great deal of stress for everyone around you.

So, what should you do when you're within these situations? Well, if you have someone who is angry and is not in a good mood, it's best to let that person get some fresh air by himself or herself. It's a good idea to run away from a situation that may cause friction or even an outright explosion. Therefore, avoidance and running away can be a good solution. Distancing yourself from people who exude negativity is also good policy. The truth is, negative people, get their energy from sucking out the positive energy out of people. They love to tear others down only to feel better about themselves. They are insecure in themselves and don't have any self-esteem, so the way they get theirs is by ratting away at someone, complaining, gossiping, and other ways. Negative people will almost always have something to complain about, so perhaps a good idea to get them going on something that is not their hobby high-horse of negative talk is by changing the subject. If a person is getting emotional or angry or depressed about something, you should offer to change the subject within a conversation to something a bit more light-hearted, fun, or enjoyable. That way, you and your interlocutor can have a more fun time and benefit from having happy times together. Instead of walking away, you can stay and get your interlocutor to feel positive about something that he or she loves. Find something that is passionate or exciting to talk about, and you will see how enthusiastic the situation will become.

Negative people are tough to deal with. They are not always easy to be around and cause you a lot of stress and strain. It is best to find ways of changing the subject, avoiding, or even running away from them because they will suck the energy and life out of you. Think about whenever you have a great project that you want to do, and you're really excited about it, and you tell your friend, who tells you not to try it because it's not worth it. Then, the wind in your sails is taken out, and you feel depressed and discouraged. Don't let negative people bring you down. They want to do it, and they will do anything to get after your positive and upbeat emotions. Also, they want to turn it around and make you feel bad about yourself. It can be a good idea to avoid that person if you can.

Let's look at an example of how to handle a negative person.

Joe is a person who continually complains at the office, and he invites people into his gossip about coworkers and his boss. He goes out drinking every night until 5 am and loves to talk about how much of a good time he has had the night before. He tends to yell at you whenever he finds something, he disagrees with you about and gets fired up. One day, he had a conversation with a coworker named Daniel. They talked and talked, and Joe was getting riled up about something, and Daniel said, "let's talk about something else." So, they continued to another topic. But then Joe started yelling at Daniel for another topic. Daniel said, "I should be going actually. Sorry, I have an appointment." Daniel then left the conversation. Eventually, Joe's negative energy was sucking the life out of the office, and he was fired after a long haul.

How was this dealt with?

Daniel realized he wanted to be a good friend and listen to Joe and talk but also knew how negative and emotional Joe could be. He tried to change the subject of the conversation to something that was not so sensitive and then it backfired. Joe then got emotional, and Daniel left. Later, Joe was fired, and his negativity must have had something to do with the situation.

Conclusion

What can we take away from this discussion on extrospection? The way to truly relate to others is to understand how they think and feel. That involves analyzing how they think, feel, and react to different situations. This is the way to understand best where a person is coming from because the way to truly be relational is to understand the feelings and emotions of different people. Emotional sensitivity is very powerful these days with the extensive play of Facebook and how people interact with people on the web. It can get gruesome at times online because people find ways to tear each other down and say truly awful things about others online, even though many times, they would not behave that way in real life. However, the thing is, with communication on the Internet, it has made it easier than ever to make emotional responses. In addition, it exacerbates the situation, because often, people are made stressed or angry from what they read online.

Reading other people's emotions is an essential skill to have when you are focused on others. You learn what makes people sad, angry, or happy, and it can be great in bringing people together. But it can also make people go in opposite directions. It is vital that you find ways to relate to others through the emotions, because it enables you to have a spiritual connection with another person, almost like kinship in which you talk about something together, and it stirs in you an emotional bond that can lead to close friendship. This is not to say that all close friendships operate from this perspective, but it means that emotions are essential to bringing people from different background together to share in experiences with one another. When you can connect with another person's emotions, then you can bring out the best in the other person and find ways of interacting that are meaningful and productive.

Finally, it is essential that we move to be others-centered in our extrospection. Being aware of our own emotions is important, but it is vital that we move to how we relate to others and form relationships so that we can have a good time with our friends, coworkers, family members, or anyone else who is in our circle.

Part II: Introduction

Four Week Emotion Intelligence Booster Program

In this section of the book, we are going to go into how you can enhance your emotional sensitivity to help you hack your way to getting that promotion and success in your workplace. We know that you want to get ahead where you work, and we want to give you the tools to do that. So, we are going to provide you with a step-by-step guide to raise your emotional intelligence (EQ) and give you the right tools to enable you to be successful in your goals and aspirations for your life.

Let's begin with the emotions themselves. Choose one emotion for every four weeks that you want to work on. Begin with the basic emotions, and then you can move on to the more subtle and advanced emotions as you go along. We want you to go through each emotion one at a time. Moreover, for every emotion, you will take four weeks. If your intended goal is not reached for each emotion, you should repeat multiple times the exercise. Throughout your journey, we advise you to keep a journal of your thoughts to record how you're doing with it.

In the next chapter, we will highlight each step of this journey that you can take to get on your way to better emotional intelligence. We will show you how you can use this knowledge to your advantage, as you seek to be a better employee or manager within a company. We hope that this information will be helpful to you, as you try to understand the emotions better. In each part of this journey, we will guide you through the ups and downs through different anecdotes that will illustrate our points. So, let's go on this journey together.

Chapter 4: Week 1: Intro- Basics- Self-Awareness

At the beginning of this journey to emotional understanding, we should begin with how you experience emotions and your way of recognizing them. You have to become self-aware and examine how you are experiencing emotions from day to day. It all begins with self-regulation of the emotions.

How Do You Recognize the Emotions and Feelings Within Yourself?

One way to be self-aware is to write down your thoughts that you experience from day to day. Get a journal and start writing down all your passing thoughts, especially the ones that are causing you stress or anxiety. You should learn how to recognize when you are feeling angry or sad and take note of what you think triggered or caused this negative emotion to come about.

You should think about how you are reacting to each situation. For example, if you were angry, perhaps you became enraged and started shouting or throwing something. Alternatively, if you were sad or depressed, you went to your room and cried it out. Another example is that when you got the news that your friend was getting married, you immediately jumped up and down and started shouting. Once you have gauged how you responded to each situation, then you can evaluate how you responded to the scenario. Think to yourself: "was this an appropriate response?" "Did I act out in the right way, or could I have responded differently and more positively?" Or, perhaps, you experienced a positive emotion that helped to solve a situation. For example, maybe you were able to solve a problem yourself that you thought was really difficult, then you discovered there was a simple solution and could laugh it off and think that it was no big deal. Often, we can learn to laugh at ourselves; it can help us to have more joy and peace in our lives. It is also a part of self-acceptance that enables you to reach your goals and accomplish the purposes of your life.

To fully understand, how emotional regulation works, we have to look at some concrete examples of self-awareness.

Negative Emotional Reaction Example 1:

Immanuel was often a perfectionistic worker. He tended to be hard on himself and at times would self-flagellate as a result of the mistakes that he made. He had very high standards for his life because he had attended a renowned university with an honors degree and knew that he could accomplish all the purposes for his life. Like many people who were high achievers, his perfectionism made it hard for him to deal with the negativity that inevitably would enter into his mind at times. Immanuel constantly dealt with the fear of failure and "imposter syndrome." This would infiltrate into his work at the office as a paralegal at one of the leading law firms of Boston. Immanuel was a big picture INFJ man, who often liked to look at big ideas rather than details. Although he had a good deal of detail-orientation, he tended to make small mistakes that he would internalize and self-implode after recognizing them. He would get stressed and worried about it. One day, he was doing his daily data entry tasks, and he was swamped doing it when he realized that he had cut off a whole field of data and that it got lost. He was mortified at his mistake and was fearful, anxious, and deeply sad at what had happened. Immediately when he made a mistake, he became depressed and was very upset at what had happened. He didn't eat for a few days afterward and cried at home because of his mistake. He also became worried and experienced a flood of intrusive negative thoughts that caused him great stress. Eventually, he was able to correct his error, which was a slip of his attention, but he was greatly worried about his job and whether or not he would get punished for his action. His boss told him it was no big deal and that this was just one mistake that he had made and that it would be okay.

Was This Response Appropriate?

It was ok for Immanuel to feel sorry about making a mistake. However, the extent to which he responded to the situation went overboard and caused him stress and anxiety. He entertained the negative thoughts that flooded into his mind after the incident. In addition, he internalized the negative emotion, which was not properly dealt with and so he was suffering quietly. He was not able to externalize his negative emotion properly, so he became depressed.

How Could He Have Responded Differently?

Immanuel could have responded differently through countering his negative thoughts through some emotional regulation. Instead of responding with anxiety and stress and bottling up his feelings, he could have countered negative thoughts by telling himself: "it's okay, you made a mistake. It happens to everyone. You're still a great worker and talented. You've had a lot of great experiences, and you are well-qualified for this job, but you just made a mistake." He should have tried to spot these intrusive thoughts and responded with some positive thinking. Immanuel could have also gone to a trusted friend and talked to him about what had happened. The talk therapy could help him to cope with his feelings of disappointment and discouragement.

The takeaway from this story is that to manage emotions properly; it is essential to get them out in the open, to share them with others. It is important also to note the self-coping strategy of handling negative emotions, including positive self-talk that can help a person to avoid going off into unhealthy expressions of emotions.

Positive Emotional Response: Example #1:

It is common knowledge that the best workers are those that are happiest and are the most satisfied with their work. When a person is satisfied with their work, they feel good and want to do their job. They are absent less to work due to sickness, and they are much more productive than their less happy counterparts. When a person is doing well and enjoying his or her work, then they will produce the best work possible, and it is a win-win for the employer and the employee. When the workplace treats the employees fairly, and with decent compensation, then all workers are happy. So, whenever a person is happy at work, he will do a good job. Let's give an example of a person who is happy at work and is doing a good job.

James truly enjoyed his work as a project manager at an editing company. He was passionate about writing and found it profoundly satisfying work. He wanted to produce the best results for his clients. Because James enjoyed his job, he wanted his employees to feel the same burst of excitement when it came to working on a project. So, he treated his employees fairly. He never contacted them during their off hours. He respected others greatly and didn't want to demand too much of his employees. James wanted his employees to enjoy a work-life balance and not make their lives simply work-work-work and no play.

Why Was James So happy?

Well, for one thing, he enjoyed his work. He was paid well, which makes a difference, but it is not the only factor in making work satisfying. James liked what he did and enjoyed project management, and he was good at delegating tasks to his employees. However, at the same time, he used his happiness to make others happy. James wanted his employees to enjoy their work just as much as he did, so he did his best to ensure that they were doing well by encouraging them and offering them quality feedback on their work.

What Does Happiness do for Work?

When a worker is happy, he will do a much better job in producing results. The example of James shows the productivity of an individual who finds satisfaction in his work. This is not the case for the majority of workers. Most people working are not happy with their work. They only go to work for a steady paycheck and nothing else. One article finds that ¾ (75%) of all American workers are unhappy at their jobs. That is a saddening statistic to have. And the thing is, the majority of work that people do is mundane, boring, and uninteresting. This causes many workers to become disengaged and not productive at work. But when you have one person who is deeply satisfied in his work, you see that this can affect how others also experience this enthusiasm and passion. James was aware of his own happiness as a worker. And then, he chose to give out his positive energy to others. It began with a positive experience of emotion and then led to his outward expression, which impacted his workplace and community. Positivity: it's infectious and exciting.

Negative Emotional Response Example #2:

The next example is one in communication, which is one that is very important to consider in workplace situations. Wilson is the head manager of his translation company and is in charge of communication for the different project managers. He had one issue of communication in which he did not communicate with everyone in his office and instead did a lot of one-to-one contact with different individuals. As deadlines started to pile up on people, some of the project managers were missing their deadlines, because Wilson did not effectively send out the deadlines to all the project managers. This led different project managers to get very angry at Wilson for not adequately communicating the deadlines and for only doing it one-on-one. One project manager, Amy, was visibly upset and she yelled across the room to Wilson: "You idiot! Why did you not send out the notices to the project managers?! You're so inconsiderate! I can't believe you!" Looking at Amy's example, she got agitated and became angry with Wilson for his poor communication style, but instead of approaching Wilson directly, she vehemently screamed at him from across the room to get his attention. Moreover, then, everyone in the room was shocked to see this display of emotion.

What Could Amy Have Done?

Poor communication is a crucial factor in workplace conflict and hostility. It causes friction within the most productive of workplaces. However, it can be a factor in getting people riled up with their emotions. Amy could have recognized her negative emotion and contained herself and simply gone up to Wilson and confronted him directly, but she was so upset that she screamed at him from across the room. In addition, Amy could have gone with one of her colleagues to him and talked to him about this problem and perhaps the issue could be resolved then. However, it is up to Wilson to resolve his problem of poor communication with his colleagues. He needs to get his act together. That said, Amy needs to come up with a way to healthily confront her colleague rather than exploding in emotion. Perhaps, she could have written an email to him and then arrange to have a meeting with Wilson privately. This would have resolved the issue.

A crucial part of recognizing negative and hostile emotion is realizing when you're starting to get riled up. With Amy, she needed to control herself and regulate the emotional response which was beginning to escalate over time. If she had known how to deal with her negative emotion, she would have responded more positively and dealt with the issue by talking to another coworker, confronting her manager, or writing an email. This would have aided her in coming up with ways to do this.

Positive Emotional Response #2:

In another example of an emotional response, we can see how positive emotions can influence others and lead to success in conflict resolution. Jill made a mistake in communication with her colleague. She told one of her other colleagues about a project but misstated the facts about it. Jill then communicated a different story to another colleague, and they got confused about the matter. She was very frazzled with herself over the miscommunication and felt sorry for what she had done. Instead of getting upset about the matter, however, she told herself: "everyone makes mistakes. This is the first time this has happened. I will apologize to colleague #2 and tell them the fact of the story." Jill then apologized to the second colleague and explained the real facts about the project. There was conflict resolution, and the situation was much better. Jill was able to forgive herself, and then her colleague also overlooked the situation and thought it was no big deal.

What Did Jill Do in This Situation That Helped?

Jill was a bit frazzled with herself. That is understandable, as everyone makes mistakes. However, she did not beat herself up about it, nor did she blame someone else about it. Instead, she owned up to her mistake, apologized, and then forgave herself for what she had done. In the end, she was able to move on, and her customer was too. Often, we can be our harshest critic and can be hard on ourselves. However, in this case, Jill was comfortable with herself, and she did not have a problem with apologizing over the issue and resolving the conflict of communication. It was a good result and a positive response to the emotion that she was experiencing.

Conclusion

We hope you've been able to see the importance of self-awareness and understanding when you are experiencing emotions, particularly negative ones. In the workplace conflict resolution is so essential to creating a harmonious atmosphere for all workers. There is nothing worse than when you have a workplace with hostility and alienation among the workers. When you create a positive working environment for your colleagues and subordinates, it can make the difference between a toxic workplace and a positive and upbeat company. We now want to provide you with some daily note-taking sections to guide you through the process of recognizing emotions. There will be one section for each day of your week.

Notes:

Day 1: How are you feeling today?

_____

_____

What happened today at work? Did anything upset you?

_____

_____

Were there any triumphs or success stories this week that you can write about?

_____

_____

How did it make you feel?

_____

_____

Day 2: How are you feeling today?

_____

_____

What happened today at work? Did anything upset you?

_____

_____

Were there any triumphs or success stories this week that you can write about?

_____

_____

How did it make you feel?

_____

_____

Day 3: How are you feeling today?

_____

_____

What happened today at work? Did anything upset you?

_____

_____

Were there any triumphs or success stories this week that you can write about?

_____

_____

How did it make you feel?

_____

_____

Day 4: How are you feeling today?

_____

_____

What happened today at work? Did anything upset you?

_____

_____

Were there any triumphs or success stories this week that you can write about?

How did it make you feel?

Day 5: How are you feeling today?

What happened today at work? Did anything upset you?

Were there any triumphs or success stories this week that you can write about?

How did it make you feel?

Chapter 5: Week 2: Basics of Self-Control

In this chapter, we are going to talk about how you can use your emotional responses to maintain self-control in your interactions with others. This is especially important when you are talking to different colleagues, subordinates, and clients.

Every emotion we have is a response to a situation that we come across in our lives. It is always purposeful and meaningful. There is a reason that you are experiencing a particular emotion and it is valid. All feelings are valid. At the same time, our emotional responses are what either become a positive or negative reaction to the different stimuli that we may experience in our lives. You should listen to your emotions, but you also need to learn how to regulate how you respond to them because it is vital that you have a plan in place to deal with complex and negative emotions that can be overwhelming and difficult.

One way that we deal with negative emotions is through the "fight or flight" response in which a person reacts to a situation based on their emotional reaction. They do not have time to reflect; they respond. For example, when a person is in a dangerous situation and sees a bear in the woods, his initial instinct is to run from the danger in fear. That is a natural response to the emotion of fear. Every time a feeling occurs, it is vital that you observe how you are feeling at a given time and observe how it is. A crucial step in dealing with emotions is to identify what it is that you are feeling and see if what you think reflects the reality of a situation. You must validate the accuracy of your feeling with empirical evidence.

As humans, it is challenging to regulate our feelings and emotions. However, we have the power to influence our feelings in positive ways. When we develop our emotional intelligence skills, we can regulate how we will respond to overwhelming emotions, such as anger or anxiety.

About Emotional Regulation

One of the most crucial parts of emotional regulation is recognizing the negative emotions that we have objectively. We must see that it is normal to feel one way and we shouldn't make a moral judgment against the negative emotions as if it is terrible to experience such things. Sometimes, our emotions are triggered by a sense of justice, and when we see unjust actions and behaviors, we want justice to be served. For example, if you get angry at how a person is being treated at the workplace, you have the right to get mad about it. A sense of justice can produce a kind of "righteous" anger in that you may realize that something is wrong and you want to correct it. However, what you do with this emotion matters.

Emotional regulation at work is going to help you to put all your emotions in check. You'll have to go through the process of getting your feelings in check. Furthermore, there is a step-by-step process to get there. Let's look at how you can achieve emotional regulation at work.

1. Label Your Emotion

One of the first ways you can deal with your emotion is by labeling the emotion and understanding what it is that you are feeling. This is a technique that is used in talk therapy such as cognitive behavioral therapy or dialectical behavioral therapy for people dealing with various mental health challenges. Primary emotions are the body's way of reacting to triggers that might cause a person stress. For example, if you see someone being mistreated at work and they are getting maligned or criticized by the management, you have the right to feel angry about it. You can identify what it is that is triggering the negative emotion in you: injustice and think about ways you can deal with that emotion.

Example of Labeling the Emotion

How do you label an emotion? Immediately when you start feeling an emotion, you talk about what it is that you are feeling. When you begin to feel depressed or down in the dumps, you can tell yourself, "I think I'm starting to feel down today. Maybe I should go for a walk or run and get those endorphins flowing again." Alternatively, when you're starting to feel stressed about an upcoming deadline, you could tell yourself, "I'm feeling nervous about this upcoming deadline. I think I need to get to work now."

Identifying the emotion is an essential step in the process to self-regulation because once you know exactly what it is that you are feeling and why you can come up with ways to manage the symptoms of what you're feeling. You can formulate the most positive response to the situation.

2. Letting Go

The next step in emotional regulation is letting go. As humans, we often become entangled in our emotional cycles and can't manage to pull ourselves out of it. Rather than letting go when we hold a grudge against someone, we hold onto it and clutch it like a death-grip on a steering wheel of a car. However, letting go from an adverse emotion is going to enable you to release the stress of a given situation and manage your response to a negative scenario, and then, you won't feel like you need to respond to every little thing. Here are some steps that you can follow with that.

A. Observe your feelings without judging them. Furthermore, see how the situation comes about.
B. Say to yourself: "I am feeling this emotion. I won't feel the same way tomorrow or the next day."
C. Embrace your emotions. Instead of fighting off the negative feelings, we should embrace emotions as part of our humanity, because it will help you to have a better time at coping.

Example

Whenever you're feeling you need to let go of something, you release it so that you don't think about it anymore. For example, if you have a feeling of resentment against someone for passing you over and ignoring you one day at work and feel angry at that person, you're able to let go and forget about it when it happened. Even if a person does not tell you, he/she is sorry, you're able to release the feeling of resentment and keep going with your life. It helps you to live in complete freedom.

3. Self-care

Dealing with emotional cycles begins with taking care of yourself. You have to have a healthy body to feel well each day. Also, it is essential that you take care of your health because we are not guaranteed to have healthy bodies all the time. If we feel tired, sick, or hungry, our emotions can be negatively impacted. Physical effects on our body can provoke us to feelings of anger, anxiety, or depression. One example of an emotion that was recently added to the dictionary is "hangry," which is a combination of hungry and angry. The spelling is not off, because a person may be mad because they are hungry. It is evident that no one makes good decisions when tired and hungry.

Having good self-care is going to be an essential part of your routine, and it will impact how you feel in social situations. In the workplace, it will affect how productive you are, because if you feel good about yourself and your appearance, you will exude more confidence and project that assertiveness onto others. Having good hygiene, getting the proper exercise, and eating well will be ways that you can take care of yourself, and you will feel much better when you interact with others at the workplace.

Self-care will be especially important to you as a manager at the workplace, because you will be delegating tasks, holding meetings and conferences, and other jobs that demand a significant amount of your time and energy. Therefore, it is crucial that you find time to take care of yourself, because this will influence your emotions and how you behave and interact with others at the company.

Case Study

Amanda is a headhunter of a human resources company in Atlanta. She recently got promoted to senior manager at her company. She had to invest a lot of time and energy in her job at first that it became very stressful and challenging for her. For a while, however, she was not eating and was always stressed at work. Sometimes, she would work through lunch; she slept for 4 hours at night and did nothing but work even into the night. Amanda recognized her unhealthy attitudes toward work. It was affecting her emotions. She would get frustrated at work, swear, and yell when she didn't get her way.

Moreover, she would continuously feel stressed and anxious. In the middle of her second year, she decided she would stop working so hard and get her life together. She tried meditation and aromatherapy at home. She would also take long baths at home. Also, she developed a more positive work-life balance, which enabled her to be more successful and confident at work. Later, she would arrive at work each day eager for each new task. And when she had a dispute with anyone at work, she would control herself and respond in positive ways. It created a much friendlier and more relaxed working environment.

4. Be positive

Another strategy that you can incorporate into your emotional regulation is to be positive all the time. You should enjoy the beautiful emotions that you have and not dwell on the negative thoughts that you might experience. Let yourself smile and laugh even at difficult things. You should also learn to laugh at yourself whenever you make mistakes because everyone is prone to making an error here and there. To leverage your positive emotions, you need to find the time to enjoy positivity and surround yourself with others who will do the same. Try to counter all the negative thoughts you may be experiencing with positive ones. It will make a difference, and you will notice how you come across to others.

Many managers are quite critical of their subordinates and don't hesitate to point out all the mistakes in their employees' record of work. They tend to dwell on giving negative feedback to others, and this causes a significant amount of problems, because the workers may feel fearful or worried about their performance as a result of mistakes they have made. If a manager lashes out in anger, then this will impact the motivation of the worker and lead to employee dissatisfaction and discouragement. Therefore, as a manager, you need to find ways of looking on the bright side and control your negative response to the things that your employees are doing. By being positive and exuding that positivity, you can make a difference in transforming the work culture of your company. It will make for happy workers and managers.

Example

It is critical to stay positive whenever we are confronted with particularly challenging situations. Oscar was a manager of a Fortune 500 company in the human resources department. He always had a lot to do and seemed to have a never-ending list of things to do every day, but he struggled to complete all the items on his list. He became very discouraged by it. He thought, "I'm just no good and cannot do everything. I think I'm going to fail. I'm a failure to launch." One day, he was having coffee with his colleague and mentor named James and the two discussed how each one was doing after a long day. Oscar said, "I'm struggling with negativity. It seems to be welling up inside of me. Every time I go to my task manager on my computer, I start to have this surge of negativity, and it causes me to feel depressed and sad because I feel that I will not be able to accomplish all the tasks that are assigned to me. It's dreadful. What should I do, man?" James responded by saying, "Oscar, bro, you're going to have to practice positive thinking. It's so important that you find good things to say to yourself. You need to start with saying, 'I can do this. I am capable, talented, and smart. I'm just going through a rough patch right now.'" Oscar was relieved to hear this from his colleague and realized that he was too hard on himself and that he wasn't listening to an inner voice of affirmation and positivity. After that moment, Oscar started to affirm himself. He began to give himself compliments about his appearance and his ability, and he began to feel better. He realized that being positive would be vital to him reaching his goals and completing his daily tasks, so it worked.

5. Allow Yourself to Enjoy Life

Life is too short to be so serious and focus solely on work. As a manager, it is vital that you have a positive work-life balance and encourage your employees to do the same. Go to a movie every once in a while. Treat yourself to dinner at the newest cafe-restaurant. Hang out with your friends and family. Enjoy your life. It will encourage you to be balanced, and you can also model that for your employees. By leading a balanced life with finding room for work and play, you will also help with regulating your emotions and feel happier in the process.

In addition, you should foster this spirit of fun by inviting your colleagues and subordinates to a company dinner or outing, which can give your company a sense of conviviality and enable your company to have fun with a drink or meal. This will also help regulate the emotions by encouraging positive responses to situations. Not to mention, having a meal is a proven way to help relax a group of colleagues.

With the social aspect of enjoying life together, negative emotions will not overpower you, and you will feel the difference in many ways.

Case Study

To control his emotions, James had to do things to enjoy his life. He used to be a workaholic and work 60 hours per week and 12-hour days. However, lately, he has been timing himself and not overcommitting to the tasks he is doing. Instead, he is finding ways to have dinner with friends throughout the week, go to a movie, see a soccer game, and write in his journal. As a manager of a Fortune 500 company, he knows that he must have a cheerful attitude at work so that he can be the best boss to his employees. He is also aware of how balancing your life is essential to living a healthy lifestyle. Therefore, he strives to commit himself to no more than 9 hours at the office. He encouraged others at the office to do the same. James said, "When it's 6:00 pm, go home.

Enjoy your family. Be with the ones you love. I don't want you to be workaholics and work until 8 or 9 at night. That is not healthy. I want you to enjoy your life." Work-life balance makes a big difference in how you can control your emotions and maintain stability in your health.

6. Worry Less

To avoid getting caught in the trap of a negative emotion that can disarm you, you should focus on the positive and practice uplifting self-talk that will enable you to get out of anxious or worrisome thought patterns. Admittedly, we have a lot to worry about in our lives, whether that is in finances, relationships, customers, or a number of other things. When you worry less about stuff, you will have less emotional responses that are negative to the various difficult emotions that we face.

Example

Yannick was a person who was a worry wart. He always seemed to have something to worry about all the time, and he especially got concerned during tax season and the time to pay his bills. He struggled with the finances of his small business. It was their first year in business, and things were going forward, but Yannick was struggling to pay off debts and bills that seemed to pile up endlessly. Because of this new business, Yannick was forced to think about money and how to operate his company seemingly all the time, and it was a real struggle to get through at different times. Yannick wanted to seek professional help for his emotional situation, so he saw his financial advisor who also did therapy sessions, which enabled him to get out all his worries about money and to feel good about everything. His financial advisor told him, "Yannick, you need to stop worrying about your financial future. Planning is everything. When you have everything planned out, you won't need to worry anymore about it. Everything will be settled. What I want you to do is stop worrying. Your emotional cycles get out of hand whenever you start worrying. You need to simply stop the thought and divert your thinking to your successful future." Yannick realized it would take time to train himself to not go in that direction of worrying about his business and financial future, but he stopped worrying and was able to reach his goals. After a year, he was able to stop worrying so much and lived a life full of joy and peace, because his financial advisor believed in him and his ability to overcome the hurdles that were in the way of his life. It was a success story.

7. Notice When Your Emotions Start to Get Out of Hand

When you start to feel the problematic emotions overflowing, you should respond to the situation. As we have suggested, you should journal about these experiences and write down all that you are feeling at a given time. Remember how you react to different situations and recall how you were able to solve different situations before. Then, you can correct your emotional response to things later on.

Example

An example of seeing when things are getting out of hand is Kelly. She was a hair stylist operating her own business in Central Square in Boston. She also managed the other hair stylists in this business. Kelly tended to complain a lot and to critique her stylists and their abilities and sometimes she would get angry and go off at them in her office whenever they made a mistake. She would always yell at them and show her anger to them in private, whenever the customers were not there. Little did she know, Kelly had an anger management problem, which had multiple causes. For one, she had broken up with her boyfriend who cheated on her for a long time and then told her. For another, she was resentful of her friends who were already married, and she was still single, so there was a lot of bitterness in her heart.

As Kelly learned emotional regulation from her mentor, she realized that she needed to stop herself before going off the edge. Whenever she felt she wanted to spill her emotions on others through her tirades about customers and difficulties, she had to stop herself before it got out of hand. Kelly became more self-aware as time went by and then she realized when she needed to stop herself from going off at people. So, when she felt she was about to get angry at someone, she would stop and sit in her office alone and give herself about 10-15 minutes to meditate in the silence and quietness of her heart. It helped things so much and then she was able to feel the difference of it.

8. Hit Your "Pause" Button and Stop Yourself

We all get furious over something that happens and yell or scream when something does not go our way. It is human nature. That said, one thing that you can do in practicing self-control is hitting your "pause" button. You stop in the middle of what you're doing. Observe what is around you and in your immediate surrounding. Take a deep breath and close your eyes before you respond to a given situation. Moreover, then, after this pause, you can return to what you are doing and can effectively manage the situation.

For any management situation, it is vital that you have a "pause" button to help you take a time-out before you get emotionally wrapped up in a situation and react negatively or regretfully. Exercising emotional self-control is an essential step to your developing as a person and manager of a company.

Case Study

Bill was a senior project manager at Apple Care products in San Diego, California. He was organized, helpful, and friendly. One thing that irked him was whenever his employees were late to a meeting. Once he got enraged and blew up in front of them and said how irresponsible and uncaring the employees were. After learning how to control his emotions from watching videos from seminars on emotions, he was able to learn how to manage himself and hit his pause button. Instead of lashing out at his late employees, he took the time to collect himself and then made a joke out of it to lighten the mood a bit. He then talked about the importance of punctuality. Later, he followed up with a company email that stressed the importance of being on time to meetings and that he was not going to let down on it. To motivate his employees, he chose the strategy of saying that he would make the meetings much shorter if the employees would come on-time. It worked and then the employees were happy and wanted to come on time. However, this happened as a result of emotional regulation and control, as well as influential people skills that motivated the employees to do the right thing and follow company instructions.

Conclusion

There are many different ways you can develop self-control in your emotions. Emotional regulation is one of the most important things you can do as a manager and as a person because the way you handle your feelings is going to speak volumes about your character and personality to others. If you're able to contain yourself and your feelings, rather than acting on emotional impulses, such as by yelling or throwing a temper tantrum, you will demonstrate a sense of maturity that will be a model to your employees. No one wants to work for the boss, who is moody and scares his subordinates into doing what they need to do. They want to work for someone approachable, friendly, and sensitive to the emotions. As we have mentioned above, emotional intelligence has a higher value over IQ, because when you connect with people, it has more meaning and significance than if you were to be smart and know all the answers. While having the brain power makes a difference and is useful, it is more important that the manager has the interpersonal skills to resolve conflict, handle various difficult situations, and manage the emotions of the people around him or her.

We hope you have been able to note all the ways that you can exercise self-control in your workplace. We want to give you more space here below to reflect on what you have learned and put it into practice. Here are some more journal pages that will help you get started.

Notes:

Day 1: How are you feeling today?

_____

_____

What happened today at work? Did anything upset you?

_____

_____

Did you react to any situation in a particularly negative way today?

_____

_____

If yes, how could you handle the situation differently in the future?

_____

Day 2: How are you feeling today?

What happened today at work? Did anything upset you?

Did you react to any situation in a particularly negative way today?

If yes, how could you handle the situation differently in the future?

Day 3: How are you feeling today?

What happened today at work? Did anything upset you?

Did you react to any situation in a particularly negative way today?

If yes, how could you handle the situation differently in the future?

Day 4: How are you feeling today?

What happened today at work? Did anything upset you?

Did you react to any situation in a particularly negative way today?

If yes, how could you handle the situation differently in the future?

_____

_____

Day 5: How are you feeling today?

_____

_____

What happened today at work? Did anything upset you?

_____

_____

Did you react to any situation in a particularly negative way today?

_____

_____

If yes, how could you handle the situation differently in the future?

_____

_____

Chapter 6: Week 3: Intro: Basics to Recognizing Emotions in Others

Welcome to Week 3! You're already well into half of the program already and are prepared to tackle your next project, which is recognizing emotions in others.

Suppose that you and your spouse are having an argument at breakfast over who will do the household chores in the evening. Your wife or husband is furious and gets very angry over it. You can read it in their face. Immediately, you feel the sensation of it as you're about to walk out the front door. It is raining buckets outside, and you get out in the rain, and your dress or suit get caught out in it, and you get a massive stain on it. When you arrive at the subway station, there is a delay for the trains, because there was a runaway train on the tracks. So, you wait for 20 minutes. You realize you're going to be late to an important meeting where you're going to give a sales presentation about your company's signature product. You are anxious and nervous at this point. Once you arrive at the office, there is a fire drill, and all employees had to leave the building, so you have no time to prepare your PPT, which was supposed to go on the screen fifteen minutes ago... everyone goes back into the room. There is a state of dismay and discord among the people there. Your colleagues and employees are sitting in the meeting as you're giving the presentation. They are bored out of their mind and looking at their phones. You can read it on their faces that they are not buying into what you want them to know, so you feel quite disappointed with this. So, you go home and sulk with a bottle of wine.

This situation was an emotional day for you. First, it started with you recognizing your own emotions and respond to the stressors that were aggravating you. Then, you were able to read the cues of the people around you, while at the meeting. This is a sign of emotional recognition in others that you should take care to examine as you are becoming more aware of others' emotions.

Reading people's emotions is one of the most important things that you can do in understanding others and their reactions to different situations. The Mayer-Salovey-Caruso-Emotional-Intelligence-Test: MSCEIT Self-Development Workbook by Susan David and Jim Grant presents many different methods that a person can work with to regulate emotions and recognize emotions in others. It includes a chapter on emotions. Whenever you read others' emotions, you can pick up on cues that people are making with their body language and facial expressions, and it allows you to understand how a person is feeling.

Some have said that a lot of what we can pick up on about others is through nonverbal communication and often that is by looking at different expressions on people's faces to let us know how a person is feeling. In the MSCEIT Self-Development Workbook, there are several different passages on how to read people's facial expressions to let you know how a person is feeling at a given moment. Many decades of research have been given to studying facial expressions and have shown that 43 muscles in the face produce a given expression (Grant and David). These muscles can be connected to the different emotional expressions in people. One way that we can use facial recognition is by telling if someone is lying by their face. It is a natural inclination that people have.

On the other hand, there are professionals at the FBI, who are trained in lie detection to spot fiction amid truth. Some people can read the emotions of others better than others, because of the way that a person has been raised. For example, they might have picked up on feelings of sadness, because they had had many traumatic experiences as a child of losing loved ones or pets. Therefore, they would be more apt to recognize the emotion of sadness in others.

Here below, we will look at different emotions, as they are presented in the workbook to give you a feel for how to do facial recognition in people.

Recognizing Emotions in a Person: The Basic Emotions

Happiness is an emotion that is shown in different ways. That said, a lot of it appears within a person's eye. It includes upturned corners of the mouth and a grin on the face. A happy expression on the face also has oblique eyebrows, and the edge of the lips is pulled straight down. The mouth also has a curved look. Often, with this expression, a person is looking down at another person. Sometimes, you can tell if a person's smile is a social smile to conform with rules of politeness or if they are genuine smiles. For example, when a person smiles with a social smile, the skin around the eyes will not wrinkle. Often, it takes a lot of practice to decipher if a smile is genuine or not. Some are easier to spot than others.

Example in Your Life

The way that you will be able to tell if someone is happy is by a genuine smile. For example, imagine you are the CEO of a company, and you are happy to give a promotion and pay raise to your employee. You have a big meeting, and you extend the offer to your employee and can immediately sense their excitement. The person lights up with joy, and their positive energy comes flying back at you. Their smile is infectious, and their voice is loud and responds with a resounding "yes! I will extend my contract! Thank you so much for this promotion! It's fantastic!" When you experience this moment as a CEO, it will make you feel joyful and satisfied in your role of rewarding excellent work and providing your employee with valuable opportunities for advancement.

Sadness

Sadness is displayed on the face through a curving in of the eyebrows and upward toward the middle of the brow. The eyes are not concentrated and are looking out into space. An expression of sadness can quickly be taken for one of shame. It is not an expression that is easy to fake. You can even try to fake a sad face in the mirror, and you will find yourself unable to look at yourself without laughing. If you are not trained well, it will be quite tricky to look truly sad in the mirror. However, there are some emotional manipulators, who use tears as a way to fake sadness. Some people can do this, and force tears out of their eyes. It is essential for you to look at a person's eyebrows to find a genuine expression of sadness.

An example in Your Life

Imagine for a minute you have an employee, who is working for you and they recently lost someone special to them. Perhaps, they lost a grandfather, or even a mother or father.

Their situation must deeply sadden them. If you have empathy for those who are hurting, then you will extend kindness to this situation. You will sense a person's sadness by the way they look you in the face, and you see the frown or low and downcast look.

Moreover, you will detect it. Once you do, you should do your best to help the person to feel better. When you show empathy to someone who needs it, then you will be able to handle the pain along with the other person and share in the suffering of another. It's something that every manager needs to know how to do because it is a potent force that can connect two people through shared suffering and struggle. Empathy in this situation would probably only be genuinely achievable if you had gone through a similar situation, such as losing a loved one. However, when you can identify the emotion in another and offer some consolation such as "I'm sorry for your loss" or "I'm thinking of you," it can help another person feel a lot better about the situation. Just being there and saying nothing can help, because empty words can often hurt a person more than being silent.

Fear

Widened eyes usually indicate the underlying emotion of fear with the upper eyelids and the lower ones tense up. The eyebrows also come together and turn upward with the lips extending horizontally toward the ears. When a person is afraid, their eyes are not open wide like in a surprised look but rather the mouth is stretched out sideways. The lower eyelids also are pulled tight, and the whole face looks more tense than usual. In addition to the facial elements, fear also has several physiological factors that influence how we feel, including blood circulation to the legs that makes us ready to run out the door.

An example in Your Life

Fear is an emotion that many people experience in their lives every day, and it is something that you should recognize in yourself, as well as in other people. Fear can easily cripple employees of different companies, who fear for losing their jobs due to some error that they make or due to cuts in funding that cause numerous layoffs. As a manager, you have to be sensitive to the emotions that your employees may be experiencing. Say, your employee makes some mistake in data entry that causes a problem and a person in Publication Quality Assurance (Pub Q/A) spots it. They also see that there is not only one mistake but many mistakes on the same form. This employee named Annie realizes her mistake and immediately displays a white face with shock from what she has done. Her mouth is open having realized what just happened and she is both fearful and surprised, a combination emotion. You see it and know how she is feeling at this time, so you try to console her and tell her to calm down. She is getting into panic mode. Her heart is racing, and her breathing is shallower and faster.

In this situation, it is best for you to find ways to console your employee. Let them know it was a simple mistake and that it can be fixed, but you should also warn them that it cannot happen again. Giving a warning is necessary for extending grace to the other person when they need to have a second chance. Having an emotional sensitivity to realize that everyone makes mistakes and to be kind to your employee will also help them in their emotional state to get better.

Anger

Anger is an emotion that can be recognized on the face relatively quickly. There are different degrees to which a person may become angry, due to frustration, indignation, or other factors. When a person is angry, their face will indicate a slight physical urge to propel forward at another. This makes a person feel threatened by the face of a person. The most obvious sign of anger is the narrowing of the eyes and a squinting face. This facial feature enables a person to focus on the target of their anger. In addition, anger has a variety of physiological effects including blood that flows to a person's arms.

An example in Your Life

Anger manifests itself in a variety of ways, but you will usually see it in the form of frustration with people that are unhappy about something. It can also be in the form of a complaint. You can detect a person's anger by their tone of voice and looking mean and threatening. For example, you might have an employee, who is angry at the computer for being slow or not booting up properly. You see him banging on the desk, shouting curses at the computer such as "Come on, you piece of junk computer!" It is obvious when a person is experiencing an angry spell, and it is essential to be careful to handle it, as it can be quite aggressive as emotion and sometimes, people do not know how to control themselves. Therefore, exercising emotional sensitivity is a valuable skill to have when handling someone who is angry.

Let's look at a concrete example of an expression of anger within a corporate setting.

Say, one of your colleagues is late for work and is texting in meetings, and your boss notices it and gets angry at him or her. She becomes incensed that your colleague could be so rude and proceeds to have a shouting match with him or her at the coffee place of the office. She shuts the door to the place and continues to berate that person for a full five minutes. Everyone can hear it from the back of the office and are surprised at what's happening.

Why was she angry? Clearly, it was because the colleague had shown rudeness in tardiness and texting during a meeting. This escalated the problem and then she became utterly enraged by the situation and wanted to let it all out, so she proceeded to get into a shouting match. It didn't end well from that moment on.

Disgust

The emotion of disgust can be seen whenever there is wrinkling of the nose, the raising of the upper lip, and other factors. It often indicates when a person is not happy with a particular smell that they can sense. They will also turn their head away from the situation. Disgust is an emotion that is too easily recognizable in a person.

An example in Your Life

The workplace can be a place of negativity and griping and complaining. Furthermore, you will notice people being disgusted by their boss's behavior and treatment of different people. For example, they might see their boss treat one of their employees to coffee for doing a good deed and then when they do a similar thing; they might get nothing. Special treatment and doing favors for others is something unfair and will make a person complain a lot. This expression would be disgust that a person would display because of the preferential treatment that is shown. Disgust is something that should be avoided in the workplace because it creates hostility and can put a rift in different kinds of relationships.

Surprise

Surprise is an emotion of instinct that a person will experience automatically when caught off guard. We are automatically trained to be alert of our surroundings all the time. Surprise typically lasts briefly and is a response to something unexpected. As it is a fight-or-flight emotion, it tends to propel a person forward. This emotion is a more complex emotion in that it can lead to other emotions. For example, if a person receives a letter informing them, they owe $2,000 to the government, they might be shocked and surprised and then consequently feel sad and disappointed. Another example might be if you received a tax refund in the mail that you weren't expecting, you might feel surprised and also happy and excited about that.

Typically, a surprise is indicated by a brief instinctual response and involves raising of the eyebrow and opening of the mouth. The eyes might be widened for a fraction of a second. There might also be horizontal wrinkles within a person's face. Surprise is something that does not last very long, so you have to be quick to see it.

An example in Your Life

Surprises come in all shapes and forms, but within the office, it could be an unexpected rush job that comes out of nowhere. Suddenly, you have to rush to complete a task that would have taken you twice as much time to do, but you have to do it immediately. Rush jobs tend to happen in publishing and editing businesses, where writers and editors must rush to complete an assignment. These are often high-stress positions that require the immediate attention of the worker. When a person gets a surprise rush job out of nowhere, they might hit the panic button, realizing that they have less time, or they might get excited and yell "Yahoo! I'm going to get double time pay for this job!" Surprise rush jobs have a mixture of thrill (happiness) and fear (nervousness) because you experience the rush of adrenaline that hits you when you receive the request and accept it on the computer screen. But then immediately after, you think, "OMG, how am I going to complete this assignment on time! Shoot! I have two days to complete it. How the _____ am I going to do that?!" Surprises are quite exciting but also dreadful in the sense that they can lead to feelings of exasperation or fear immediately afterward.

More Complex Emotions at Work

Happy for Someone vs. Jealousy

This kind of emotion can go both ways, depending on the person, because a person may be both happy for another person and also jealous of them. For example, if a colleague gets promoted at work, you might say to him or her, "I'm so happy for you! It's great that you have this amazing promotion. I'm sure you'll do a great job." Sometimes, you might say such words, but inwardly, you're wrestling with feelings of jealousy at your coworker's promotion, because it shows your inadequacy as well as their superiority. For this emotion, you might see a fake smile on someone's face indicating that they are happy for you, BUT they are also quite jealous of you, because you are effectively showing that you are superior to them and that by getting this promotion, you will make them green with envy, because you can talk down to them. It, unfortunately, creates a dividing wall of hostility between you and your colleague. So, you must be careful in how you approach such a situation.

Let's look at a concrete example of how this would work for you.

Case Study

Keith has worked hard at his job. He has always turned in his tasks on time or before the deadline, and he has also stayed late at the office and even come in early on some occasions. Although soft-spoken, Keith also likes to talk about his work and what he is doing, and this can make his colleagues jealous of him. They say to themselves in a somewhat gossipy way: "He can't shut up. He always talks about work. I wish he would get a life. I don't enjoy my work half as much as he does." On the other end is Thomas. He works just as hard as Keith. He goes into the office early and leaves late. That said, he makes some mistakes in his work, because he is a newbie to the office, yet he has the experience of Keith, with three years of management. Keith gets a promotion one day, and then Thomas says to him, "Oh wow, Keith, congratulations, I'm so happy for you!" But you can feel that Thomas is jealous of Keith. There is something in the handshake that indicates that he is jealous of Keith and perhaps even wants him not to succeed.

Awe

The feeling of awe is a complex emotion because it involves two emotions, surprise, and fear, so awe can be a bit difficult to describe when a person is feeling it. However, think about when a big CEO is invited to your dinner party at your company. Say, hypothetically, that we invited someone like Satya Narayana Nadella, CEO from Microsoft to the company dinner. He is going to be the keynote speaker at an annual conference on technology, and you will be attending this dinner. You just so happen to sit next to him at the dinner party. You have feelings of nervousness, fear, and some anxiety. However, when you look at him, you're in awe of whom you're talking to. You're talking to the CEO of Microsoft for goodness' sake! Let out a shout! You want to say: "pinch me!" But you cannot contain your sense of shame and embarrassment, because you are a subordinate, a no-name without any accomplishment to your name. Then, you sit down with Nadella, and he wants to play down his achievements. He says, "what's your name again? Tristan. Nice to meet you, Tristan. What is your job? ..." You realize that Nadella is looking at you. He sees that you are in awe of him, but he deliberately tries to downplay his fame and bring everything down to earth. It shows the humility and humanity of a person, who has much power and influence, but it is an excellent example of how a person can be inspiring but also a person who can bring everything down to one level.

This example illustrates how important it is to have some horizontality to relationships because not everything can be about subordinates and superiors. There need to be moments where everything is brought down to a relational level, where everyone is equal. Furthermore, it also shows that a person can recognize the sense of awe that is usually attached to someone who is famous and has power and influence.

How do we know that Tristan is in awe in this situation? Perhaps, his mouth is open wide, and his speech is quite fast and nervous. He may also be trembling in this situation. Clearly, the Microsoft CEO recognized this emotion in him and was able to empathize and help him to talk on the same level, which helped the conversation go smoother in the end.

Why did Tristan feel in awe? He realized that he was in the presence of someone famous, which made him recognize his inferiority and thus a feeling of shame came over him but also, he was quite fearful and respectful of the presence of this famous person.

Shame or Embarrassment

The feeling of shame or embarrassment can happen at different moments of a person's life, and they may feel a combination of remorse, sadness, and even surprise at times. You will know if a person is embarrassed based on how they look at you. They may look down and feel bad, or they might even turn red in embarrassment or a modest way. Shame is a sensitive issue because it is something that causes many problems in Eastern cultures, where a person is expected to save face at all times and never show a particularly strong side of themselves. This is especially the case in Korea or China, where saving face is a crucial part of life.

We all know someone who has demonstrated shame whenever they were unusually confident. Imagine a student in a class blurting out the wrong answer, and his face turns noticeably red, or his heart starts racing. This is a common occurrence, and it is essential that the instructor has a good deal of empathy for the student and not make any moves to embarrass a student.

This type of emotion can also be expressed in the professional workplace whenever a person blurts out an off comment in a meeting and turns red in the face. Let's think of a situation where we're in a meeting at the office, and one of the employees is making a presentation.

At the presentation, the employee named Ted has his PPT all ready, and he puts his USB into the drive on the computer in the conference room. He has all his files ready and then, all of a sudden, the monitor screen doesn't work, and Ted has a hard time opening the file. Something else is wrong: the file is corrupted and is making an error message happen, so Ted will not be able to open the file, unfortunately. He will have to make the presentation by himself while using a whiteboard and marker. Ted's face starts to turn red as a result of the embarrassment that he has experienced. He sees everyone there waiting for him to talk, quickly texting someone on their phones while muttering to each other. His heart rate starts to rise, and his body temperature is also going up, as well. As Ted made his presentation, he continued to have a racing heart rate, and he was sweating buckets afterward too. Everyone looked at him and were quite unhappy with what he had done. Ted had made a negative impression, and he could feel the eyes of everyone in the room, which were like needles that were piercing his soul from their unforgiving and hostile gaze.

How do we know that Ted was embarrassed? Because he was turning red in the face and we can tell that he was becoming agitated and shameful because the technology was not working and causing him problems and made him look bad in the meeting. Because Ted also felt dismayed as a result of this experience, he made many blunders as he was making his presentation. This caused him to feel bad about having made a poor showing in front of his colleagues and superiors. It was a difficult time for him. His manager saw how he was doing and followed up with him the next day. He told him that he understood that everyone has a bad day and that this was just a one-time experience. It wouldn't happen again.

Contempt

Contempt is a more complex emotion that involves looking down on another for a mistake they had made or for appearing inferior to another. It is an emotion that can be experienced whenever you have certain coworkers that may be looking down on another, because of a handicap or other matter. Contempt is an emotion that is felt among many people and yet is one that needs to be dealt with maturely, because workplace abuse is often a problem and can cause many issues for workers.

Let's give a concrete example of this. Say, you are working for a telecommunications company, and you have a person who is on the team who has a mental handicap. He is just a little bit off. Often, he talks to people in the office, but has a speech impediment and sometimes does not know what is socially acceptable to do. He has sometimes tried to hug someone to show love and affection. The person who hired him realized that he had a handicap and that he would need to have some accommodation for his mental disorder.

However, the team has its share of people who want to gossip about this man named Johnnie. There are quite a few people that like to mock him behind his back. When they hear him talking, behind his back, they laugh and carry on and joke around about him. They say things like, "can you believe he said that? He is such a jokester! I can't believe he is like that. He needs to get a life."

Intervention into this type of situation would be important for a manager because contempt can be something that people feel for another person; however, the manager needs to recognize it in them and know how to deal with it. Let's see how the manager dealt with the situation.

The manager decides to write an email to company members (excluding the named person). The email reads:

Dear colleagues,

I hope you all are having a good day. I am writing to talk about Johnnie. I know that he is an integral part of the team and that he works hard to do his best for our company. He has been made fun of by several people, not to mention any names. I've heard of people laughing behind his back in the office when I went to get coffee, and I have to say, it has got to stop. *Showing contempt for your fellow worker is inhumane. It is disgusting, and I do not want you to continue in this way. It is unnecessary. You need to treat others with respect and the way they want to be treated. Johnnie has a mental disability and needs to be given the proper accommodation for that matter. I know how much he contributes to our company. I would appreciate your cooperation in this matter and that you would stop talking about him behind his back. It is not right. I will not hear of it again. If you want to talk to me further about it, please let me know.*

Thanks, and have a great day.

Best regards,

Michael Crafton, CEO of Warner Telecommunications

Anticipation

Anticipation is a complex emotion involving excitement and expecting something to happen, and it is something that many people will be looking forward to, especially when it comes to getting a day off from work. Most people in America work for their holidays and look forward to the time when they can leave work and travel to a deserted tropical island to get some R&R. You can feel it with your colleagues as they are anticipating the time when they will take their vacations. It can often infiltrate into the office, as people are coming expecting their next time when they can have time off from their jobs and spend time with their friends and family.

As the workday goes on, you can experience how people are getting ready for the vacation season to begin. They are at their computers doing their jobs, but sometimes they may feel distracted because they are thinking about what will happen in the future. Therefore, they think that they cannot concentrate on their work. This can also be the case when you have people who are

Relief

Relief is a feeling that you may experience as a complex emotion in which you will feel relieved from a situation that has caused considerable anxiety or stress only to realized that it is not as bad as it had seemed once before. A person who experiences relief is usually quite happy and surprised but also in a peaceful mood. Relief is something that many people experience on a day to day basis. Often, a person is anticipating something that is going to happen before. They are waiting for an undesirable outcome to happen and then are surprised by the fact that it doesn't happen. Therefore, they experience the emotion of relief, which is an emotion that is a "pleasant surprise."

Let's look at a couple of examples of this in a corporate setting. Harry is working at a high-tech start-up, and he realizes he has a deadline with his external provider that must take place very soon. Unfortunately, Harry has procrastinated some on this assignment, so he starts to feel panic as soon as the deadline approaches. He reaches out to his external provider, who is in charge of this assignment to find out if he can extend the deadline. It had been given to him on a very tight schedule that he had to follow well. He was starting to panic and to think, "There's no way in _____ I will be able to achieve this, I need to talk to someone now." Before he started to panic, he contacted the external provider about the deadline, explained the situation and then said, "Could you please extend the deadline? I'm in a desperate situation, and I don't think I can finish on time." The external provider named Ted said, "Sure Ted, no problem. We found out that there is no rush on this assignment. So, you're free to turn it in when you can." As soon as Harry heard this, he was filled with relief. He was able to breathe easier and helped him. You could see it in his face as he exhaled a deep breath and his face lit up with life and peace. It meant that he was able to relax again and get back to work so that he could finish the project in good timing.

Satisfaction

Satisfaction is an emotion that experienced when a person has happiness and peace in their life. It also has to do with a person's motivation and their ability to complete a task efficiently. To feel satisfied with one's work means to think that you have done all that you could do to complete a task and now you can rest in the job well done and submit the task. Imagine that you have a person who is working on a high-quality translation assignment at an in-house translation center. Call him Dave. Dave is a highly proficient in-house translator working on a high-profile translation job for the UN. He has worked for a long time on it and has submitted it to editing and proofreading, and it has taken about a week to go through that process. Once it has completed that cycle, Dave takes a look again at his effort that he has exerted on the translation. He has spent well over 40 billable hours on this assignment, which is going to earn him top dollar for the translation. As he is working with a high-profile client, the UN, he knows that he is going to get a reasonable payment for his effort. So, having completed his assignment, he knows he has done his best. He has had experience with this kind of job before, so he knows of his potential success rate and has confidence it will go through well. Therefore, he experiences satisfaction. He can sleep well at night, and he is calm and at peace.

The Power of Verbal Communication: It's All in the Voice

There have been studies that have shown that the voice is a more critical indicator of emotional expression than nonverbal ones. While you may think that you know what a person feels when you observe their nonverbal cues and signs, these signals may not be an accurate depiction of what emotion a person is experiencing. However, according to one study by the American Psychological Association, voice-only recognition is a more precise indicator of a person's emotional state, as evidenced by multiple experiments with different strangers interacting using only their voices.

The voice is a powerful instrument that communicates through the different inflections and tones, which makes it a reliable indicator of a person's emotional state. Think of how a voice projects whenever angered or irritated. The voice allows you to recognize if a person is feeling exasperated, excited, sad, and so on. All six of the basic emotions can be detected using this method. Through voice-only recognition, a person can listen carefully to another person without other cues. When a person cannot see another person's face, they are forced to rely on the sense of hearing, which allows them to be acutely aware of the sound of another's voice. Therefore, it is crucial that you pay attention to another person's voice when they are talking because it can help you understand whatever emotion they are experiencing at a given time.

Case Study

Charles was working in a telecommunications company as a customer service agent, and often, he was on the phone with customers resolving various situations, including disputes that would occur every day. He would be on the phone all day with customers in the call center and had to talk to people all the time. As an introvert, Charles struggled with self-confidence and approaching others, who were around him. This was also the case for his telephone encounters. Over time, Charles became an expert in detecting how people felt over the phone. He could tell when a customer was angry at him by the inflections of their voice and the high volume with which they were shouting at him. He knew immediately when they were enraged at the new company's policy. Alternatively, in some situations, he would hear the nerves of the customers when they were talking to them about an exorbitant roaming charge that a customer received for using the Internet while in a foreign country. The high-pitched voice that included shallow breaths clearly showed the signs of fear within the person who was speaking to him. You could also hear the desperation within the customer's plead for mercy. Additionally, Charles received calls from customers who wanted to express gratitude for resolving an issue. In their voice, you could hear the sigh of relief, and utmost thanks as breathing resumed as they talked to him. Often, you can intuitively sense a person's emotions just by listening. It can be easy to "feel" a person's emotion based on the energy that is being emitted from a person's voice. After all, we can feel the power of a person's voice, which is quite angry at another. Also, we can feel the emotional reaction of a person, who is anxious and crying because of some external cause.

Conclusion

To sum up, we have been able to show you the different ways to identify people's emotions based on both the facial expressions as well as the inflection of a person's voice. As humans, we are hard-wired for emotions. Moreover, as we have been able to deal with our own feelings, we can also be ready to handle other's emotions, as well. You see it at the workplace all the time. The expression of emotions is everywhere. Also, it is vital that we find ways of understanding how people are feeling and why people are feeling that way, based on their emotional experiences. As we deal with others' emotions, we can respond in the ways that are constructive and helpful. Emotions are a powerful thing that we have to gauge how people are feeling. This will help you to manage people better, if you are a manager and to get ahead in the workplace. It is important that we connect with each other's emotions on a personal level because that enables us to form deep, lasting connections with people that are meaningful and productive.

Emotions can be first recognizable by our facial expressions and how we show our faces to others around us. Often, it is the visual sign that displays the heart and how we feel about someone. No need to express it verbally, just orally. A visible sign and body language will demonstrate our true feelings about others in our workplace. Therefore, it is vital that we find ways to understand others' opinions and how they express their emotions through the visible signs and cues that we see on their faces and using their hands.

Likewise, emotions can be recognizable based on the tone of voice that a person adopts. You can often hear the emotion more clearly when you listen to the person who is having the emotion, and you can literally hear the anger, frustration, elation, anticipation, and other emotions in their tone of voice. Research has shown that specific emotions can be recognized even more acutely and accurately from just listening to a person rather than looking at their face. Hence, you can tell a person is really feeling anger toward another on the phone and you're also able to handle it when you talk to them.

Finally, emotions are a part of understanding others' personality and interests. It is vital that we develop an awareness of how people are feeling and be sensitive to their needs and desires before we can relate to them. Practicing empathy is a vital part as we show our respect and love for our fellow human being by being relational and helpful. It is essential that we do this to form ties that will bind us together for the rest of our lives. This aspect is especially crucial in people as they develop working relationships with each other.

Notes:

Day 1: How are you feeling today?

_____
_____

What feeling did you notice in others today as you were working?

_____
_____

What kinds of emotional reactions did you notice in your peers today?

_____
_____

How could they have handled it differently?

_____
_____

Day 2: How are you feeling today?

_____
_____

What feeling did you notice in others today as you were working?

_____

_____

What kinds of emotional reactions did you notice in your peers today?

_____

_____

How could they have handled it differently?

_____

_____

Day 3: How are you feeling today?

_____

_____

What feeling did you notice in others today as you were working?

_____

_____

What kinds of emotional reactions did you notice in your peers today?

_____

_____

How could they have handled it differently?

_____

_____

Day 4: How are you feeling today?

_____

_____

What feeling did you notice in others today as you were working?

_____

_____

What kinds of emotional reactions did you notice in your peers today?

_____

_____

How could they have handled it differently?

_____

_____

Day 5: How are you feeling today?

_____

_____

What feeling did you notice in others today as you were working?

_____

_____

What kinds of emotional reactions did you notice in your peers today?

_____

_____

How could they have handled it differently?

_____

_____

Chapter 7- Week 4: Intro: Basics: Social Skill

You've done it! You've reached the last week of our course in emotional intelligence. Now we can talk about the previous part of the integration of this knowledge in your daily life. This week the main focus is after recognizing and understanding emotions in people and why they happen. In this chapter, we will talk about how to react the proper way to other people's feelings. We will talk about listening skills and give good examples of this. We also will discuss empathy and stress within the workplace. Finally, we will indicate to you the proper ways to react when angry, upset, and stressed.

Learning to React the Proper Way

Now that we have looked at all the different examples of emotions that you may recognize in the workplace environment, we can talk to you about the proper way to respond to these emotions. You should know when the right time is to react or ignore a situation because it is essential that you get the balance right whenever you are doing it. Often, people get into an emotional frenzy and react automatically without thinking and are unable to exercise self-control in playing down their emotions and then allow their emotions to take over their life. This creates a dangerous situation for anyone involved because once the emotions take over, anything is possible, and you might have a relationally disastrous consequence of the action taken.

As we have mentioned in Chapter 2, self-control is a crucial step to getting you to manage your emotion so that you can regulate your various emotional responses to a given situation. You should learn what it is that makes you angry and how you usually respond to the case so you can gauge what you need to do to address the same emotion the next time you have to deal with it.

Learning to react the proper way is going to involve you overcoming your pride and thinking that you know all things about the situation. Pride has too long caused the downfall of many men and women. Moreover, it can cause many problems in your life if you're not careful. Too many of our emotional responses come from a pride-based mentality that believes that a person knows everything and everyone else is stupid and wrong. Unfortunately, we think that way. We believe we are always right, and other people are wrong, and that is why we get into an emotional frenzy whenever we are disturbed by something that is bothering us. So, you should learn to exercise humility in all things.

Where does this humility come from? It comes from a place

where you realize that your feelings are valid and that it is okay to feel the way you do but also that you might have something wrong in your assumptions, behavior, or other things within a situation. Developing humility will be an essential part of getting you into a place where you accept that you are not always right and that your assumptions and judgment may be clouded by wrong ideas that you should correct and modify your thought patterns and other things.

It will undoubtedly take you a while to fully adapt to new situations and to correct your actions, but step by step, you will be able to reach your goals so that you can do the right things and give the proper responses in situations that cause you stress.

Let's give an example in the workplace of reacting the proper way.

Let's say that you get an email from your boss that says she would like to see you tomorrow morning. No indication that it will be anything special, but then you might be wondering if it is serious and if there is something more that you need to do. Maybe you are in trouble? You might get fired. But you stop yourself from going there. If you went that direction, then you would immediately stop yourself and say, "you know what, I don't think that there is anything wrong in this situation. My boss just wants to see me. No problem here. Therefore, I am not going to worry about it."

You clearly responded well in this situation. While you could have gone off the deep end and started to worry and get anxious about a situation that perhaps had no grounds for worry in the first place. Instead, you decided to put the thought out of your mind and concluded that the situation required no immediate action other than to comply and go to the meeting.

Controlling your emotional response is going to take intentional training of your mind so that you won't go off the deep end and get yourself into relational troubles from responding in negative ways. When you react appropriately to a boss's request without going into a hypothetical struggle with your mind, then you will be more at peace with yourself and your emotions and be able to handle any stressful situation that you may be in. It will help you to do well at whatever it is that you do.

Developing Good Listening Skills

In the workplace, an essential thing that you need to acquire is good listening skills. It is crucial that you listen to others with attentiveness and understanding because that will make all the difference in building good relationships with others. Listening is a skill that is often overlooked and underestimated in our society because much is placed on a person's ability to speak well in front of others, but not enough attention is given to how we listen to others and give them our attention.

Listening is essential because we develop our sense of understanding of others' emotional needs and wants when we listen to what they have to say. Too much in our society makes us drown out the sounds of each other. We are on our phones all the time. Even in a coffee date with someone, we may be texting others at the same time or even take a call during a meeting with someone. So much that we do is just plain rude, especially in social situations. That said, we are also living in a society that is plagued by people who have ADHD, whether that be clinically diagnosed or not. Regardless, our attention is so short and limited, so we don't listen to people the way we should, and that gets us into a lot of trouble.

One way that we get into a lot of trouble is through the misunderstandings that we have as a result of not listening. It can be relationally destructive. Imagine that someone hears something that you said, and it was not meant to be offensive, but the other person heard something else, so it hurt their feelings. It can put a rift within a relationship and can cause anxiety and hurt on both ends of the spectrum.

Let's give an example of this in the workplace. Jacob and Jane are colleagues. They have a good working relationship, but sometimes they get into misunderstandings of communication, and it causes both of them stress and anxiety. Jane has given her concerns to Jacob, and yet he doesn't seem to listen to her and their communication together. He thinks everything is okay and that their relationship is good, but she insists that there is a problem and that it needs to be fixed. Jacob realizes that he is wrong and apologizes. He says, "Jane, I know I have not been listening to you, and it has caused you some emotional pain. I'm sorry about that. I realize that I am not listening to you. I am on my phone all the time, finishing up a task, or just simply not keeping my head on straight. That said, I'm genuinely sorry. Can we meet again on Friday to talk about the project?" Jane forgives Jacob for his blunders and seems to put it behind her. She responds with: "Sure, Jacob. No problem. I understand you're busy. However, you also need to learn to listen to others, because that will help you to do better."

Jacob was a jerk to Jane. He was missing meetings, not communicating properly, and causing great frustration in the working relationship. But as soon as Jane confronted him, he was able to hone up to his mistake and made a difference in his action, which was quite positive and enjoyable. Therefore, he was able to make adjustments in his habits and acts which make a difference to his life.

Listening is an essential skill in communication because it shows a vested interest in someone else. When you listen to someone, you're showing the proper respect and honor that a person deserves to have. Playing on your phone, texting another person, or even taking a call during an important meeting is blatantly disrespectful to a person's time and is also going to cause emotional difficulties between persons. Therefore, it is vital that you find ways to listen to others and show them the respect they deserve because otherwise, you are showing dishonor to them and it is absolutely ridiculous. It is vital that you do this and that you are careful to do all things well.

The people that listen well are those who are typically reserved and don't like to talk too much with others. Introverts, in general, seem to fit this type of profile. People who listen more than they talk are the ones that do the best with this type of task and can provide the kind of emotional stability that is needed within a relationship. Introverts are people that are not necessarily unsocial, but instead, they adapt themselves to social situations so that they can listen to others and give an ear to hearing from others. They are emotionally sensitive in many cases and can be good listeners to hear you out whenever you're having emotional difficulties.

Extroverts can be good listeners too, but often, they are so wrapped up with what they have to say that they don't take the time and energy to listen to what another person is saying. While the interlocutor is talking, extroverts can concentrate so much on what they have to respond to that they forget how another person is talking to them and this causes disgrace to them. It is vital that you find ways to help others by listening to them and caring for their needs before your own. Thus, an extrovert can learn a lot from an introvert by learning how to withhold their thoughts until listening to what another person has to say because that shows respect and care. It also demonstrates a great deal of emotional maturity that is necessary.

Let's look at another example of workplace listening that is crucial to your success in a company.

Sam was a very enthusiastic worker and was full of questions that he wanted to know everything there was to know about his job, so he would intervene whenever he wanted. At a meeting with his coworkers, he was always the one to ask questions. While everyone sat there and were mindlessly on their phones without looking up at the speaker, he was taking notes and actively seeking answers to his inquisitive questions on the topic of the day, which was Python. Most other people in the room were not interested and were showing that they didn't care about the speaker, who had come from New York for this meeting. Sam demonstrated a great deal of maturity to listen to the speaker and ask good questions of him during the meeting, which was essential to help the speaker feel welcome and valued.

After the meeting, the speaker had a coffee with Sam. They went to a local Starbucks and engaged in deep conversation together. It was great, and they became good friends and talked about Python in depth. Furthermore, it all started with Sam and his excellent listening skills at the meeting at his company. He showed a vested interest in the speaker and then went out for coffee with him. He practiced his listening skills and asked a lot of questions and the speaker developed a lot of respect for Sam. In the end, it led to the development of a relationship and the two shared each other's business card.

What can we learn from Sam?

Sam was an active listener and showed interest in someone else by developing a list of questions that would help him express his interest in the other person. He demonstrated a great deal of respect to others, even when other people showed a disinterest, rudeness, and attention-deficit behavior. In contrast, he was an engaged listener and was willing to have a conversation with the speaker after the meeting, because he wanted to get to know him more. Active listening is an important skill that helps bring people together and allows relationships to flourish and improve over time. If one person is doing all the talking and the other person is doing a lot of listening, it can be a bit too much to handle. But the thing is, we have to listen as well as speak and do a lot of give-and-take in situations. To be a good listener, we need to ask good questions, and that is what Sam teaches us. The power behind being a good listener is how to ask questions and follow up with questions that respond to what a person is saying to you. If we have the right questions, we will be able to engage with the other person and activate their knowledge of the topic at hand.

What are some good questions to ask another person?

One of the critical aspects of asking good questions is a curious attitude that listens carefully to what others have to say. So, you need to ask the right kind of questions. You shouldn't ask simple yes or no questions that demand no other response other than "yes" or "no." This will not activate prior background knowledge that is useful to help cue a person into making their response. Instead, you should use responses that include questions such as the following:

- Who, What, When, Where, or Why: These are specific kinds of questions that demand more thoughtful responses other than "yes" or "no," and require more reflection and preparation from the person. These kinds of questions are specific to a type of presentation that you do and will help you to activate the background knowledge of a person, as they are speaking to you. As a prompt, these questions will provide the speaker with the cues that they need to describe something.

- Also, make use of "How?" The question of "how" will help the speaker reflect into how something is done and will require more thought or consideration but enable a person to respond to your question appropriately.
- Ask follow-up questions. Rather than leaving your questions to open-ended or yes or no questions, it is vital that you prepare a list (in your head) of follow-up questions, which will be helpful to get you to listen to what others have to say. It will also demonstrate that you are listening to what another person has to say.
- Avoid asking the question: "what do you think about this?" This question is too general and vague and does nothing to activate the background knowledge of another person. It can also cause another person stress to think of something to say in response to what another person has prepared to say.
- When listening to another person as they are

answering you, don't think of what you are going to say. Instead, think of what kind of follow-up question would go with the answer that the other person is providing you. This will demonstrate that you are interested in them and that you want to know more about what they think about different things.

- Don't change the subject when you feel that you are not interested! You may be tempted to change the subject when you don't feel interested in what another person has to say, but if you change the subject too soon, it is dismissive to another person and can be quite offensive to them.

One of the visible signs that you are interested in a person is by the questions that you ask that person. If you don't ask enough questions or don't respond to what another person has to say, it shows that you weren't actually listening to what the other person had to say. It is rude and disrespectful. That said, when you take the time to ask questions, respond directly to what another person has to say, and engage in the topic that a person gives to you, then you will show that you care for the other person and his or her interests and all will be well within the relationship.

Genuine Empathy

As we have mentioned above, one of the critical aspects to emotional intelligence is the ability to empathize with another person, to honestly "feel" what another person is feeling and understand where they are coming from, because that brings you into a relationship with another person and will enable you to have a good relationship with others. The way to relate to another's emotions is to show empathy to him or her. That can be done by showing a person you care, but it is also through identifying with the struggles that a person is facing. It takes a step of rejoicing with a person who is celebrating and weeping or mourning with a person who is doing the same. You take all the steps that will enable you to enjoy the success of others and then understand and grieve with another person who is going through a difficult time. This is a crucial part of your emotional intelligence because you have to show that you can understand their feelings and be there with them through it. Let's give some examples of how you can rejoice with another and share in the suffering of another, which helps you to exercise emotional empathy in the workplace.

Rejoice with the Victors

We have already talked about how it is essential to be happy for someone whenever he experiences success and not have feelings of jealousy or resentment at how successful they are when you are left to enjoy your quiet and mundane life that has no substance or energy. As humans, we are always comparing ourselves to others and seeing what others have and desiring it ourselves. Unfortunately, all the social media outlets make this a problem that we are continually confronted with daily. Think of all the Facebook posts you see and witness people getting into a relationship, marriages, and babies. Moreover, you think to yourself, "why them and not me? What more is there to my life? I am green with envy." However, to an emotionally mature person, it takes having an ability to rejoice with those who are celebrating and share in the triumphs of another person.

So, when you see that a person has received a promotion at work and you are staring at them from afar, you rejoice with them. Alternatively, when you receive a compliment on your successful job performance, then you share in the victory with another person. Say, Tim did an excellent job on his recent report for a conference, and everyone was so happy to see his work and thought it was a great achievement and should be rewarded a promotion with a bonus of $500. You are pleased to see that Tim was given this achievement, but you know that you are struggling with your work. You have gotten some negative feedback on your performance and feel a bit inferior by this achievement of Tim, your colleague. You want to feel happy for him, but it is difficult for you. But then, you remember the time when you were promoted at your previous job, and you can identify with Tim's success. Although right now you're struggling because it is your first time in this company, you know that things will get better and your performance will improve. Thus, you can feel happy for Tim. In fact, you're able to rejoice with him, knowing that you have experienced the same thing in your life. So, you go out with Tim. You congratulate him and feel happy for your colleague and friend. At a bar, you buy him a round of beers so that he can think that you are appreciating his success and valorizing him for what he has done. Having emotional empathy means that you are relating your experiences with another person in a way that allows you to relate well to another's successes or failures. In this case, you were able to relate to Tim's success, because you had experienced something similar and knew how hard that Tim had worked because at your previous job, you had also known success and the fact that hard work pays off. You still feel a bit jealous of him for achieving this feat, but you also feel more motivated to work hard, with the knowledge that with hard work that your work will get noticed and rewarded by the management of the company.

Weep with Those Who Weep

On the opposite end of the spectrum is showing empathy to those who are struggling and having a hard time. Perhaps, you have encountered a personal setback and see someone else suffering from a similar situation. You can identify with the other person and their unique struggle. Say, you have a colleague, who has been working three different jobs and is always busy. He has a family and three kids that he is raising and yet, he is still finding that he is struggling with basic financial management skills. Therefore, he is struggling financially to provide for his family, and everyone is suffering. His kids are getting hungry and malnourished because he cannot afford a healthy meal. The kids get sick, and his wife can't work, because he is temporarily disabled. So, he is living in a shitty life situation, and you can understand that because you have also gone through a similar situation. Once, you were in college, and you were also struggling financially to make it through each month. You had to work three part-time jobs and had to go to school full-time.

You were overworked, underpaid and still having to perform academically at your university. Also, you were quite sleep-deprived. So, when you heard about your colleague's situation, you were able to immediately relate to his position and comfort him in this time of need. Maybe you gave him some money to support him during this time, money that would not need to be paid back because you knew that someday, you might be in a similar situation and he could pay you back for it in some other way. This is a Korean method of payment known as *Jeong*, which implies that a friend will provide for another in time of need in a reciprocating way.

What can we take away from these situations?

Empathy is a profound way of emotionally relating to another person, and it is a powerful tool to help bring people together, who are in similar life stages or have gone through similar experiences. It is useful in the workplace for colleagues to share in each other's joys, trials, successes, and failures, because it brings an element of humanity to the table that wasn't there before. Work is not all about work; it is also about building relationships with other people. Empathy is a way to get people to relate to one another in ways that build trust, emotional support, and love and affection for each other. This does not exclude love relationships, but it implies that a person can get a lot out of relationships through investing in others and sharing their experiences.

Understanding Stress

Stress is a cause of anxiety in workplaces today, and it causes people to have hard times. Work-related stress causes more people to be absent from work due to illness and also causes people to have relational difficulties. However, when people can work together amid stressful situations, they can collaborate and solve problems in tandem. Stress causes people to be relationally distant from each other; however, when people come together to solve their problems, they realize that it is easier than before to resolve situations because two or three are better than one.

Within the workplace, there are several stress factors, including finances, client expectations, job demands, and management expectations. Managing this level of stress requires a great deal of skill from the worker. He or she must be emotionally mature to handle different stressors because they can cause emotional discouragement, depression, or anxiety. With empathy, workers can understand each other and the factors that cause them stress and then they can de-stress from their work together. This often happens after work at company dinners, or out having drinks with co-workers. But it can also occur over coffee, a cigarette break, or in other ways too.

It is essential to understand how you relate to stress every day and how you react to it. Often, when you have coworkers who know what you're going through, they can help provide emotional support through the difficulty and then you can handle future situations. Finding ways to handle stress is something that requires collaboration, not just individual therapy. Group therapy has had proven benefits that enable a person to manage symptoms of their work-related anxiety effectively. Let's talk about Amy and Emma.

Example

Amy and Emma are both nurses, and they work at a hospital in Bristol, Tennessee. They work long hours and usually twelve-hour shifts. This causes their bodies a lot of physical and mental stress, because they have to be on their feet all the time, take care of the patients, witness traumatic situations, including deaths, help patients use the bathroom, and provide support to their patients. This is a very challenging situation to continually be in.

Consequently, Amy and Emma provide support to each other. They help each other throughout the day. Sometimes, they send texts to one another that gently encourage one another. Although they don't work at the same time, they try to provide emotional support to one another. On Saturdays, they meet for coffee and lunch and provide talk therapy to de-stress and discuss the week's happenings. It helps them to feel better about themselves and to encourage each other to face the challenges that they have as nurses. Being a nurse is one of the most challenging, underappreciated, and noble professions in the medical field. Nurses provide the care to the world's sick, dying, and aging population. They are the heroes of the medical world and need to have the mental capacity to handle all of the traumatic and stressful situations that they continually have to deal with because they suffer alongside the patients.

Additionally, they must have empathy for their patients, to do an excellent job in treating them for the various illnesses that they have. Through the variety of experiences that they have with patients, they develop the emotional maturity and empathy that is crucial to aiding patients who are suffering and their families and loved ones. However, they also need to have emotional support themselves and may need to have talk therapy with friends, therapists, counselors, or mentors.

How to Deal with Complaints: Is it Valid or Invalid Complaining?

Complaining is an aspect that always comes with the territory with workspaces. There are always going to be complainers who are loud and obnoxious in the workplace. You have to learn how to deal with them. One of the best ways to deal with them is to avoid them and not talk to them. If you have people who are complaining, you should try to avoid being with them, because their constant negativity is going to affect you and your overall morale. You could also try ignoring it and not talking to the other person, who is active in complaining within a situation. If it is valid complaining and it is about a justice issue or something that is not right, then it is best to talk privately with a supervisor or write an email to that person to address the situation. Gossiping in the office with other coworkers is usually counterproductive and creates an atmosphere of hostility and discomfort for everyone. If you have a valid complaint, you should voice it, but you should do something about it and talk to your supervisor about it. You shouldn't simply gossip with your colleagues and talk about it negatively. Instead, you should be proactive in doing something about it. This action shows initiative and responsibility, which are necessary to accomplish new things in different environments.

If you have someone who is complaining and you have to deal with it directly, it's best to just change the subject and talk about something else that is more productive and positive. Also, keeping a positive tone is going to help others to experience more joy in their lives. When you can give a positive spin to something, then you can help others to see life on the brighter side, and you can transform your environment into a positive one.

How to Create a Positive Atmosphere

This brings us to our next point: how to create a positive atmosphere. The way to create a positive environment is to be positive yourself. When you are confronted with a negative situation, you should counter it with a positive. For example, when a person comes to you and says, "See, Kelly, that shitface manager Jennifer was causing so much of a stir at the meeting. She was telling everyone how badly they did on the recent collaborative assignment. I hate her. She is always so negative. I want her to bust her butt on something," you can counter this with a positive. You could say: "Nelly, I understand your point of view, but you should understand how frustrated she was feeling. Jennifer was also having a bad day because her car broke down and she had to walk for a whole hour to get to work. Not only that but her purse got stolen while she was on a coffee break. You have to understand she was having a shitty day and therefore, you shouldn't judge her for it." What you did was that you created an environment of empathy for this person. You realized that your friend Nelly was complaining about her supervisor and that she was incensed at what the supervisor had done. However, you were seeing things from the supervisor's perspective and empathized. Also, you told her not to judge her. So, you were effectively negating the negativity of your colleague and making it into a positive. You could say to Nelly, "You know, Nelly, we all have bad days. It causes us to act out in ways we previously wouldn't. It's going to be okay. We have to understand each other and forgive others."

Positivity involves emotional empathy and understanding, but it also consists of looking on the bright side of things so that you can get things done more effectively. For example, say that your boss gives you a 15,000-word report that you have to do. You could feel bad about it and say, "Gah! This is terrible. I don't want to do this. It's horrible." Alternatively, you could say, "let's do this thing. It's going to be great. I'm going to learn a lot from it. Let's work together on this project, and we will do an amazing job!" Having a positive, upbeat personality is going to enable you to be a great changer in your environment because you can create that positive vibe that others will experience, and they will want to be around you more because you infuse the atmosphere with positivity. That will also be a motivating factor in getting your colleagues to produce genuinely wonderful work. It will make your colleagues want to go to work and do all the things that they have to do.

You should realize that you have more control in the kind of environment that you're creating with a positive or negative attitude. If you are always positive, you will undoubtedly cause others to feel the same way. When you are encouraging, you can build others up, and it will create a fantastic environment for you and your colleagues at the workplace. That said, if you are negative all the time, it will bring others down and build a stressed and depressed working environment, which will cause others to suffer and may make you feel better, but at the expense of others. *Schadenfreude* is real, and yet it is something that does not give you pure joy. Instead, it causes other people to suffer. Negativity, while also powerful, cannot win in the end, because positive feelings are so infectious that they light up a whole office space. When everyone is happy, then the entire office is, and people are prosperous in their work. Moreover, the entire company will be able to produce fantastic work that pays well. Managers will pay their employees what they're worth, and workers will do their jobs well because they feel respected and valued. And everyone will be positive because things are going swimmingly well.

How to Give the Correct Guidance

In mentoring relationships at the workplace, it is a great thing to be relational and emotionally aware of what someone is going through in a work placement adjustment. Say, you are a manager, and you have a mentee who is new to the company for the first time. Her name is Nicole, and she is quite nervous and unsure of herself. She doesn't know all the rules and has to learn everything from scratch. However, you are there with her to adjust to the new situation because you have the empathy to understand where she is coming from because you have also had similar experiences. Using your emotional intelligence and experience, you can effectively guide her in the direction she needs to go. When you see that she is down on her luck for doing something wrong, you can come to her and gently tell her, "it's okay. Keep your head up. You will get better with time. This is the first time you've done it. You can do better next time." You have to be encouraging of your mentee and to provide the guidance that will help her to get back up and keep going.

Emotional intelligence is going to help you to relate to your subordinates and colleagues and enable you to connect to others around you, which will help you to be a better manager of others. When you can see where others have been and are aware that you had been in the same situation, for example, as an intern or administrative assistant, then you will be able to empathize with them and provide them with the right kind of guidance, to assist them emotionally and professionally. This will significantly improve working relationships with others, as well.

When to Get Mad? When Not to Get Mad? How to Get Mad in a Civilized and Productive Way?

Being emotionally sensitive is going to help you to avoid getting too angry at work and will help you to do well at managing others and be a better manager. When you know how to control your emotions, then you can do your best to help others to achieve their dreams. If you don't have enough emotional control, then you will not know how to manage others, and they will resent or hate you for it. You will be the target of your subordinates' judgment and mockery. Therefore, exercising self-control will be crucial in this matter. If you are angry, you should be in a situation where there is a legitimate reason to be angry. For example, if you find that your subordinates are cheating on their timesheet or if they are doing a sloppy job or taking too long breaks, you should confront them about it and express your displeasure with what they are doing. They are doing a terrible job and something reprehensible, deserving of disciplinary action. It is crucial that you find ways of getting your colleague's attention in a way that lets them know that what they are doing is wrong and needs to be done away with.

On the other hand, getting angry at someone for no reason

can cause rifts in relationships that can cause a lot of problems at the office. Thus, it is vital that you get your act together and show restraint and not get angry at the smaller things that don't matter but to let things go. This will make things a lot better for you and your colleagues at work.

Conclusion

As we have talked about, it takes empathy, listening skills, and the ability to relate to others to be better at relationships. It is vital that you develop these interpersonal skills because they are indispensable to your professional life. They will make your company a place that is worth working for with happy workers and supervisors. That's the best.

Day 1: Did I react correctly to other people´s emotions?

_____

_____

_____

Did I let pride get into the way?

_____

_____

_____

Did I genially listen? If not, what got me distracted?

_____
_____
_____

Did I show empathy? Did I ask the right questions? What can I do better?

_____
_____
_____

Did I show empathy? Did I ask the right questions? What can I do better?

_____
_____
_____

Did people complain to me? Was this valid or invalid? Did I react properly?

_____
_____
_____

Did I get mad or angry? Did I show my emotions in a good way or a bad way? What should I do different the next time?

_____
_____

Day 2: Did I react correctly to other people´s emotions?

_____
_____
_____

Did I let pride get into the way?

_____
_____
_____

Did I genially listen? If not, what got me distracted?

_____
_____
_____

Did I show empathy? Did I ask the right questions? What can I do better?

_____
_____
_____

Did I show empathy? Did I ask the right questions? What can I do better?

_____

_____
_____

Did people complain to me? Was this valid or invalid? Did I react properly?

_____
_____
_____

Did I get mad or angry? Did I show my emotions in a good way or a bad way? What should I do different the next time?

_____
_____
_____

Day 3: Did I react correctly to other people´s emotions?

_____
_____
_____

Did I let pride get into the way?

_____
_____
_____

Did I genially listen? If not, what got me distracted?

_____
_____
_____

Did I show empathy? Did I ask the right questions? What can I do better?

_____
_____
_____

Did I show empathy? Did I ask the right questions? What can I do better?

_____
_____
_____

Did people complain to me? Was this valid or invalid? Did I react properly?

_____
_____
_____

Did I get mad or angry? Did I show my emotions in a good way or a bad way? What should I do different the next time?

_____

_____

_____

Notes:

Day 4: Did I react correctly to other people´s emotions?

_____

_____

_____

Did I let pride get into the way?

_____

_____

_____

Did I genially listen? If not, what got me distracted?

_____

_____

_____

Did I show empathy? Did I ask the right questions? What can I do better?

_____

_____

_____

Did I show empathy? Did I ask the right questions? What can I do better?

_____
_____
_____

Did people complain to me? Was this valid or invalid? Did I react properly?

_____
_____
_____

Did I get mad or angry? Did I show my emotions in a good way or a bad way? What should I do different the next time?

_____
_____
_____

Day 5: Did I react correctly to other people's emotions?

_____
_____
_____

Did I let pride get into the way?

_____
_____
_____

Did I genially listen? If not, what got me distracted?

_____
_____
_____

Did I show empathy? Did I ask the right questions? What can I do better?

_____
_____
_____

Did I show empathy? Did I ask the right questions? What can I do better?

_____
_____
_____

Did people complain to me? Was this valid or invalid? Did I react properly?

_____
_____
_____

Did I get mad or angry? Did I show my emotions in a good way or a bad way? What should I do different the next time?

_____

_____

_____

Conclusion

As you have seen from this book, emotion regulation plays a big part in getting you to improve your emotional intelligence is by developing self-awareness and monitoring, which enables you to see how your emotions work. By exercising self-control, you can regulate your feelings constructively and healthily. You're able to get out all the negative emotions and continue to produce positive emotions, which will naturally be infectious and helpful to others. Emotions are powerful, and they influence others in many different ways, especially the "feelers" from the Myers Brigg Type Indicator. Some people feel more intensely than others.

As a manager of a company, your responsibility is to take care of your employees, and you have to be sensitive to their needs and emotional expressions. Many times, colleagues and subordinates will get frustrated and complain when times are difficult and when work is tedious and taxing. The manager needs to address the needs of his or her employees to make them happy because a happy employee makes a happy company. It is essential to gauge the emotional level of the employees within a company because you want to create an upbeat and enthusiastic atmosphere for your employees. They should want to go to work and not dread having a case of the Mondays. You want to make work exciting, enjoyable, and profitable for your workers because then they can produce the best products for your company.

We have been able to walk you through a four-week plan of monitoring of emotions within your company. We hope you have taken careful notes in the journal and notes pages that we have created for you. Emotional control and regulation will enable you to understand people within your company and their unique personalities. It gives you a taste of how to relate to others and practice intuitive social skills. Therefore, having high emotional intelligence (EQ) will allow you to make good relationships with others in ways that you didn't before. It is important to develop people skills for any vocation or job but especially for the role of the manager in a company. You have to learn how to relate to all of your employees and treat them with respect and care. Being sensitive to their emotions will give you a quality of compassion that they can identify. Moreover, the employees will respect you more if you connect with them on a relational and emotional level.

With your knowledge of emotional intelligence, we hope you can take this information and form the best relationships with your colleagues, clients, and employees. You will receive high ratings from all the people you work with and be truly successful in achieving great things if you are more emotionally sensitive. We can guarantee that people will like you more and will respect you for what you're able to see in them, a person who is worthy of honor and respect. Finally, you can achieve whatever you set out to do because when you are people-centered and oriented around others, you will find complete happiness, joy, and satisfaction in your job and company.

Hello,

As an independent author,
   and one-man operation
   - my marketing budget is next to zero.

As such, the only way
   I can get my books in-front of valued customers
   is with reviews.

Unfortunately, I'm competing against authors and
   giant publishing companies
   with multi-million-dollar marketing teams.

These behemoths can afford
   to give away hundreds of free books
   to boost their ranking and success.

Which as much as I'd love to –
   I simply can't afford to do.

That's why your honest review
   will not only be invaluable to me,
   but also to other readers.

Yours sincerely,

Jonatan Slane

Bibliography

Burnett, Jane. (2017). Majority of workers are unhappy employees, study finds. Ladders $100K Club. Retrieved from https://www.theladders.com/career-advice/majority-unhappy-at-work

Cherry, Kendra (2018). "The 6 Types of Basic Emotions and Their Effect on Human Behavior." Verywellmind. Retrieved from https://www.verywellmind.com/an-overview-of-the-types-of-emotions-4163976

Chignell, Berry. (2018). The importance of emotional intelligence in the work place. CIPHR. Retrieved from https://www.ciphr.com/features/emotional-intelligence/

Clark, Josh (n.d.) "What are emotions, and why do we have them?" How Stuff Works. Retrieved from https://science.howstuffworks.com/life/what-are-emotions1.htm

Goleman, Daniel. (2015). Emotional Intelligence. [blog] Daniel Goleman. Retrieved from http://www.danielgoleman.info/daniel-goleman-how-emotionally-intelligent-are-you/

Grant, Jim and Susan David. (n.d.) Recognizing Emotions: A Core Positioning Skill. MSCEIT Self-Development Workbook.

Kraus, Michael W. (2017). Voice-Only Communication Enhances Empathic Accuracy. American Psychologist. 72 (7), pp. 644-654. Retrieved from https://www.apa.org/images/amp-amp0000147_tcm7-224388.pdf

Positive Psychology Program: Your One-Stop Positive Psychology Resource. (2018). Emotion regulation worksheets & strategies: Improve your DBT skills. Retrieved from https://positivepsychologyprogram.com/emotion-regulation-worksheets-strategies-dbt-skills/

Practical Emotional Intelligence (n.d.) Emotional Intelligence blog. Retrieved from http://www.emotionalintelligencecourse.com/history-of-eq/

Salazar,Alejandra (2017). "Emotional Intelligence: What is it, interpretation models and controversies." CogniFit Health, Brain, and Neuroscience. Retrieved from https://blog.cognifit.com/emotional-intelligence/

www.ingramcontent.com/pod-product-compliance
Lightning Source LLC
Chambersburg PA
CBHW060046230426
43661CB00004B/678